Supporting Children with Speech and Language Impairment and Associated Difficulties

Suggestions for supporting the development of language, listening, behaviour and co-ordination skills

2nd Edition

Jill McMinn

Continuum International Publishing Group
The Tower Building
11 York Road
London
SE1 7NX

80 Maiden Lane
Suite 704
New York
NY 10038

www.continuumbooks.com

First published by Questions Publishing Company 2002
Reprinted by Continuum 2005
Second edition published by Continuum 2006

Design by: James Davies
Iqbal Aslam
John Minett

Cover photograph by: Stuart Mills
With thanks to staff and children at Acton Park Infant School.

British Library Cataloguing-in-Publication Data
A catalogue record for this book is available from the British Library.

ISBN: 0-8264-9103-0 (paperback)

Library of Congress Cataloging-in-Publication Data
McMinn, Jill.
Supporting children with speech and language impairment and associated difficulties : suggestions for supporting the development of language, listening, behavior, and co-ordination skills / Jill McMinn. - 2nd ed.
p. cm.
Includes bibliographical references.
1. Specific language impairment in children. 2. Specific language impairment in children - Patients - Education. 3. Specific language impairment in children - Patients - Rehabilitation. I. Title.
RJ506. S68M33 2006
618.92′855-
dc22 20050377806

Typeset by BookEns Ltd, Royston, Herts

Contents

Acknowledgements

Thank you to all the parents who have shared their experiences with me; their worries when things were difficult and their joy when things went well. You have given me a valuable perspective and taught me a lot. The time spent in teaching your children with speech and language difficulties has been extremely enjoyable and rewarding.

I owe a great deal to all those colleagues in education and in health who have supported me in developing various ideas. Particularly the group, including Jane Williams, Gill Britten and Kate Wyke, who have helped me introduce a new way of working in partnership with our parents that is proving most successful.

Introduction

By the time children start school at the age of four or five, most of them are fairly well organized. They have sorted, classified and categorized information into the right places in their minds. They can use language to communicate and socialize. They can use language to learn.

'PE worns out me.'

This book is about a different group of children; children who are disorganized and quite overcome by disorder. Children who can't make sense of the world. They are totally distracted by all the information presented to them, so much so that they can appear not to be paying attention or even to be deaf. In fact, they are often paying too much attention to one word or phrase, trying to make sense of it, while the rest of the sentence goes unheeded.

'My dad went hammer and hammer bang went wood down.'

These are children who are lost in space and time. They can't recall the sequence of things, don't know what day, season or year it is, and are confused by *today, yesterday* and *tomorrow*. They muddle *up* with *down, behind* with *in front, right* with *left*. They can't visualize their own space or their own body moving in space. They misplace their belongings. They are clumsy, losing their balance. They may not be able to co-ordinate several things at once. Their timing is always off.

'I feel look not book reading now.'

These are the children who know what they want to say but whose language comes out muddled or unintelligible.

'On Saturday next tomorrow I will went.'

They talk about 'aminals', 'hopsitals' and 'spickets'. They say '*Mrs Minn I've shifin*' instead of '*Mrs McMinn I've finished*'.

They have a lot to say but it is impossible to decipher what they are telling us.

'Tom nursery has gone.'

They can quickly complete tasks and want to describe what they have done, but it is very difficult to follow their description and consequently they cannot easily demonstrate knowledge and understanding.

They know what it is to feel wet yet call wet things 'dry', they call breakfast 'dinner' and horses 'cows'.

'Him not got a throwinger.'

They won't accept broken biscuits because a biscuit is supposed to be round, and they may freeze when faced with a choice of two things – unable to select one.

They get bound up in the detail rather than seeing the whole.

Language is central to learning and to life in general. It helps to shape the daily routines of health and welfare, as well as social relationships in the family, at school and at work.

Language is so tightly woven into human experience that it is scarcely possible to imagine life without it.
Steven Pinker (1994)

In the school setting everything is dominated by language, from formal lessons in the classroom to games in the playground with friends. Speech and language are used to give and get information, give instructions, make friends, make jokes, express feelings. A child who has difficulty with language is therefore at a great disadvantage, particularly in school where others may be unaware of the problem and do not therefore make allowances for the child's difficulties.
JPDF ICAN (2000)

This book offers information, guidance and examples of good practice to teachers, classroom assistants and parents working with children who have speech and language difficulties. With appropriate help, these children can be taught to make their speech clearer, improve listening and co-ordination skills and to make more sense of their world. When they are given opportunities to develop and show their knowledge, children with speech and language impairment can and do learn.

The first six chapters explore how speech and language impairment (SLI) may present, and how this affects curriculum teaching within the school. In my advisory work I receive many requests for help with assessment of SLI and for setting targets for individual educational plans (IEPs) and this new edition now includes a photocopiable, task-based assessment pack in Chapter 7, and a suggested structure for IEPs with a bank of possible targets (Chapter 8). Holistic working is essential in special education – Chapter 9 discusses how best to work with parents. Appendices include a range of practical information and photocopiable material. The Books and Resources section has been fully updated and includes further reading and a range of useful contact addresses and websites.

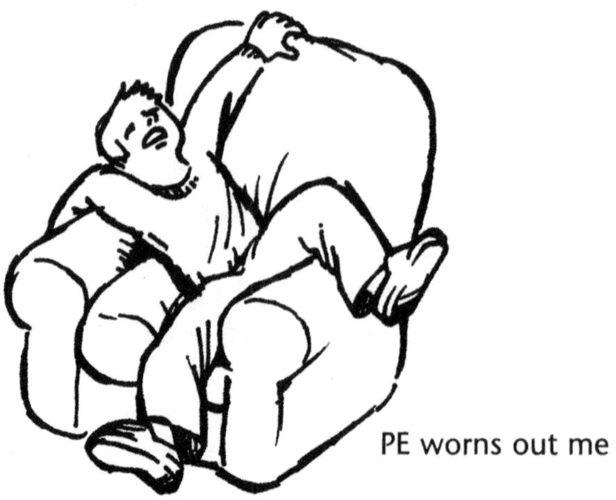
PE worns out me

Language is not solely a means of communication; it's also a powerful cognitive tool, serving as a means of mental representation, hence influencing thinking and memory
Morag Donaldson (1995)

1 What is Speech and Language Impairment?

Joy Stackhouse describes speech and language impairment (SLI) as:

A developmental disorder characterized by the late appearance and/or slow development of comprehension and/or expression in a population of children who are otherwise cognitively, emotionally and physically intact.
(Stackhouse 1997)

The NHS Centre for Reviews and Dissemination suggests that 6% of children will have some kind of speech, language or communication difficulty at some stage in their life. David Hall (1996) suggests that 1 in every 500 children will have a severe long-term difficulty.

This impairment may be called 'severe' because its effects are widespread, impeding communication and learning. It may be called 'specific' because it may not be linked to any other major difficulty. However, the term can encompass a wide range of difficulties, some of which stand on their own and some of which are also associated with other conditions and areas of special educational need. (See diagram over the page.)

Not all pupils with speech and language impairment will attend a specialist class; a significant number will be in mainstream classes. Many Key Stage 1 teachers believe that they have steadily increasing numbers of pupils with some degree of speech and language impairment, certainly with poor listening skills. This may be so, or we may be getting better at recognizing these difficulties. Depending on how it is defined, estimates of the prevalence of speech and language impairment vary between 3% and 15%.

The number of potential cases of children with speech and language impairment is high. A conservative estimate suggests 1–2% but well-designed studies suggest 7% may have some kind of speech and language impairment.
(Law, J. *et al.* (ed) 2000)

So we are talking about a wide range of problems experienced by a significant number of children. Some of these children will be considered as speech and language impaired, others will be experiencing more general difficulties with learning, and some will have speech and language difficulties as part of other identified impairments such as hearing loss. Some of these children may spend a short or a longer time in specialist classes, others will be in mainstream classes for most, if not all, of their education. It is important, therefore, to raise awareness of these difficulties and provide some ideas of how best to support children in mainstream schools.

Children with speech and language impairment are a challenging yet stimulating group to work with. To be successful in teaching them you need enthusiasm, patience, flexibility and a large bank of ideas. The resources we have collected and developed may therefore be useful to mainstream and to specialist colleagues who work with children who need support in a range of areas:

1

- expressive language: speech, vocabulary, grammar;
- receptive language: listening, following instructions, memory;
- social use of language: behaviour
- developmental co-ordination difficulties.

Speech and language impairment can encompass a wide range of difficulties

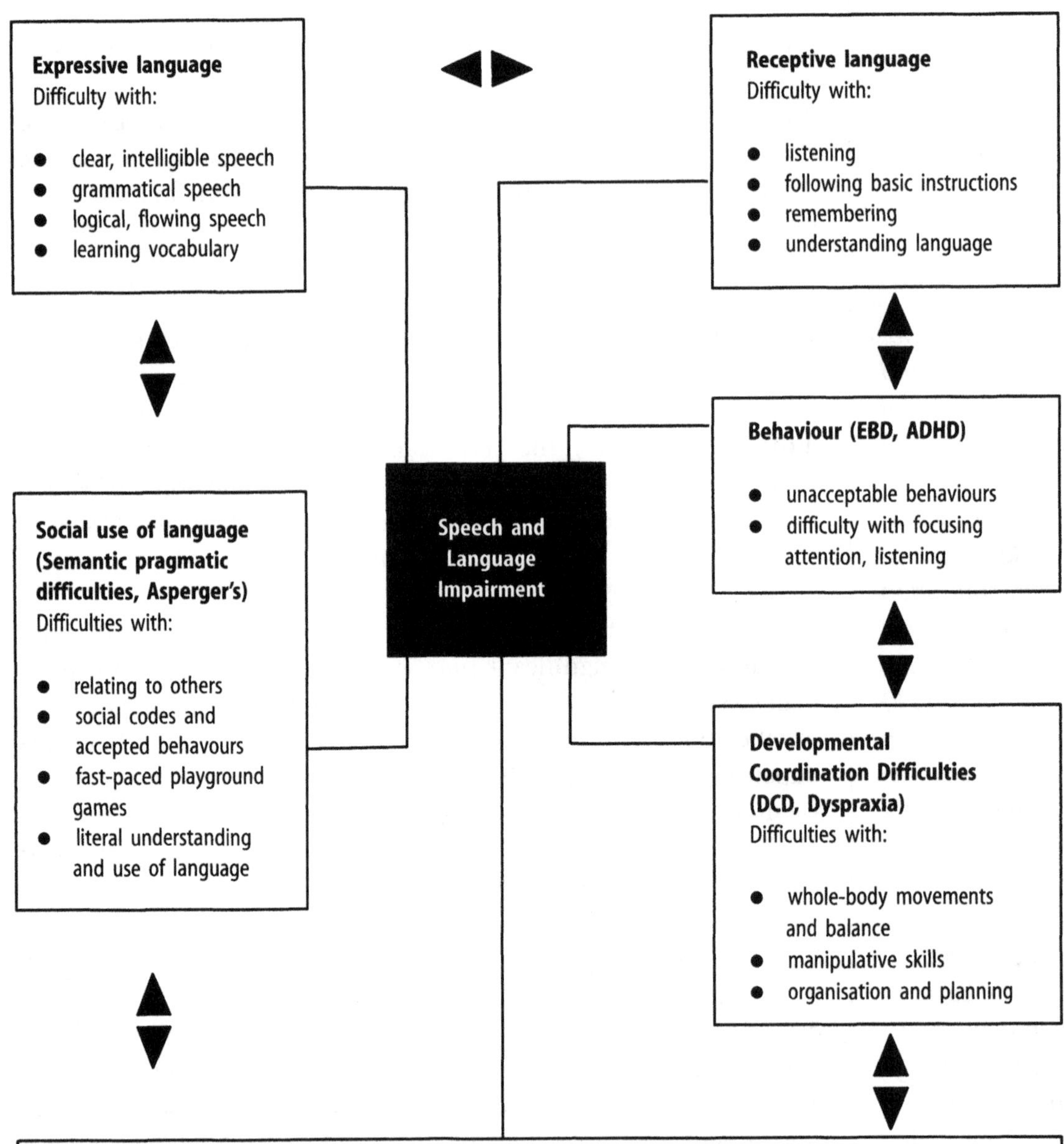

Sensory integration difficulties

- visual: problems with tracking, shifting gaze and interpreting by looking
- auditory: problems with locating sounds, identifying and discriminating between sounds
- taste and smell: over- or under-reaction to particular tastes and smells, leading to restricted diet and dislike of 'hands-on' activities
- tactile: over- or under-reaction to touch, dislike of hair or nails being cut, lack of awareness of nose running or food spilled on clothes, fiddling with everything
- vestibular/proprioceptive difficulties with balance and body awareness

2 Expressive Language

Speech production, vocabulary and grammar

2

Children with expressive language difficulties may be very difficult to understand. They may:

- use speech that is unclear or garbled;
- talk too loudly or too softly, too quickly or too slowly, hardly at all or not at all;
- use very few words and lots of gestures;
- miss out words or invent words;
- muddle or misuse syllables within words and words within sentences;
- muddle pronouns, tenses and questions;
- have trouble recalling certain words, saying nothing or using a word that sounds nearly the same or one that means nearly the same thing;
- lack the understanding of conversational rules and, though eager to have a conversation, make little sense whatsoever;
- be unable to make links and connections with language and therefore be unable to explain or describe clearly;
- give unexpected answers, since they may interpret words literally;
- lack understanding of social rules and codes.

'ga go gan?' (Can I go in the sand?)

In a busy classroom, children who have just one or two of these difficulties may be overlooked. They may give yes and no answers when questioned directly and may talk infrequently but be considered as merely shy or reserved. Children with more severe difficulties are easier to identify.

'Mrs McMinn the water bowl is stuck and it's a flood.' (Mrs McMinn, the sink is blocked and there's a flood.)

Whether experiencing minor or severe difficulties, such children will need direct support to acquire and use language.

Speech production

The children with speech production difficulties are fairly easy to identify because they are difficult to understand and may even be totally unintelligible. Sometimes, family members may learn to understand their own child in context, but such children probably still remain unintelligible to other people, including their teachers. If they cannot make themselves understood it is very difficult for them to learn alongside their peers in a mainstream class. They may have associated difficulties with the structure of language and they may go on to have literacy difficulties, more commonly called specific learning difficulties (SpLD) or dyslexia.

These children need a very specific programme of therapy to enable them to learn how to articulate speech sounds. Single speech sounds must be explicitly taught, followed by blended sounds as they occur in different positions in words. Speech and language therapists often teach pairs of sounds (c/g, t/d, p/b) that are made in the same place in the mouth but one is softer, less stressed than the other. They may talk about *loud* and *soft* sounds, and *long* and *short* sounds. They will usually practise sounds in isolation (/p/ then with open vowels pee/ pay/poh/pie ...) then with another consonant at the end (peed/ paid/ pohd/pied) and so on. They will encourage good posture and breathing throughout.

'Me not play her, her rough.' (I'm not playing with her, she's rough.)

2

This sounds straightforward but it is extremely hard work. Most children need to go over and over aspects of this work before it begins to be automatic. They do not automatically know how to shape their mouths or where to place their tongues, and often they have to slow right down in their speech production while they do these things. The children have to take some responsibility for their own improvement and to want to make their speech clearer. This is a mature concept for very young children.

When a child is working on articulating particular speech sounds it helps to work with the speech and language therapist (SLT). Within a specialist language class the therapist and the teaching staff will plan and work together. In mainstream settings, it would be immensely helpful if a key worker in school could work with the child for a short time each day; this could be the SENCo, class teacher, NNEB or classroom assistant. The therapist will have very limited time available for each child and will probably ask parents to help as well. She will usually set out a detailed programme for the child and it is clearly of most benefit if daily practice is possible. (It is useful to know the order of acquisition of sounds for speech so you can follow the SLT programme with more understanding and also to see what stage your pupil(s) have reached. See Appendix 1.)

Practice

It takes a lot of practice and encouragement for a child to carry over what has been introduced in a therapy session into free speech. If you are aware of the programme and, for instance, know that a child has been practising an initial /c/ sound, then every time 'Can I ...' is used you can be ready to encourage the use of this sound. Similarly, when reading with the child, you can expect, encourage and praise the use of target sounds.

In addition, look for times in the course of regular school activities when you can practise the target sounds in ordinary talk. This sometimes means employing techniques more often used with much younger children, such as prompting, restating and expanding what the child has said in a supportive way. Try to praise good attempts, rather than concentrating on correcting errors, and help the child to feel relaxed and happy enough to repeat target sounds in regularly used phrases in class. Sometimes it is appropriate to link speech work with alphabet, spelling and reading tasks in class. Be ready to do this but discuss it with the therapist first.

2

Be prepared for the times when you will not understand what the child is saying and be ready to acknowledge this and to reassure the child. It is pointless to pretend to understand, as the child will know you don't. Better to be ready to say:

- 'Can you show me?'
- 'Can you draw it for me?'
- 'Children, can you help? See if you know what John is saying.'

'Ta, ti to too toiti?'
(Can I go to the toilet?)

Sometimes other children are really good at interpreting because they are on the same wavelength. (Of course the child needs to feel relaxed and the class needs to be geared up to supporting him; it has to be done in a friendly, supportive way.)

- Whatever the outcome, praise the child for having a try, but if you have not understood, say something like, *'I'm sorry I couldn't understand. You are working really hard to make your talking clear and it is getting clearer all the time.'*
- Then try and have a talking time with a shared and familiar context as soon as possible, e.g. do some art work together, read together or play a game together so you can have a successful conversation. Of course this will not be possible every time but it has to happen enough to motivate the child to become intelligible.
- Give extra encouragement to pupils with speech difficulties with regard to their reading. As you tune into their speech you will be able to assess if they are reading the words accurately. Start with a core sight vocabulary, as you probably do anyway, before using 'sounding out'. (See the First Words listing Appendix 2.)
- Consider using a phonic/alphabet system that uses auditory, visual and kinaesthetic clues such as Jolly Phonics. Accept a best effort from your pupil with speech difficulties. This is where you need to liaise with the SLT, but also enable the child to show what he knows through using pictures or letters.

If a child stutters there are some ways you can help:

- Don't focus on the stuttering or label the child as a 'stutterer'.
- Don't ask him to slow down or think about what he is saying.
- Do give him time and attention, with the same chance to talk as everyone else in the group. Listen to what he says and answer or comment on the content, not on how it was said.

- Do notice which situations seem to worry him the most and consider how to overcome these.

Your speech and language therapist can give more detailed advice. Children who stutter can be lacking in confidence, and very vulnerable, isolated and subject to name-calling and 'put-downs'. (A useful and informative resource is produced by the British Stammering Association.)

Generally, in the area of speech production, you can help by including some rhythm work in your music lessons. How we speak – the expression and inflection we use – is linked to our sense of rhythm. Many children with speech and language difficulties have a very poorly developed sense of rhythm. Tapping out different rhythms and a steady beat to different songs or music, and playing softly and loudly, or fast and slow, can be fun and helpful. Rhythm and rhyme go well together so you could also choose some words or rhymes that include particular speech sounds that a pupil is working on and say and tap these. This also gives a chance for some positive affirmation to your pupil about his speech work. (Some rhymes are given in Appendix 3.)

Rhythm games

- Clapping round circle. First child claps once, then next child and so on, like a ripple. This requires good looking and focused attention and aims to develop group identity, and the group working together. If the children get good at this, make it harder by using two or more claps or a clapped rhythm.
- Tap children's names, topic or curriculum vocabulary or phrases from songs. Have these written and the rhythm marked in some way, dots or musical notes.

  Say and clap the rhythm of the words three times, whisper and clap, then think and clap.

  Or say and clap hands, say and clap knees, say and clap thighs, say and clap the floor. Then repeat this pattern but say and clap hands, then think and clap knees, thighs, floor.
- Leader claps a rhythm and children echo it back. When they are confident at this introduce 'Don't do this'. Have a card with the words 'Don't do this' and the rhythm shown in some way, dots or musical notes. Now if the children hear this rhythm they don't echo it.
- Play tap, tap say – start a rhythm, tapping knees twice then stretching hands forward in front to mark a pause. When the children have got this rhythm then introduce saying a word in the pause, taking it in turns round the circle. These can be on a given category – vehicles, food, colours – whatever you wish to work on. The aim is for no duplication, although at first it may be necessary to accept some duplications. It is useful to practise by counting round the circle or saying own names to get the feel of it first.

'I wan go girs gu egun moogi.' (I want to go first but everyone's moving.)

- Use a large dice, throw it, then clap the number.
- Use well-known rhymes and songs to emphasize rhythm. Pound fists or clap hands together on stressed words.

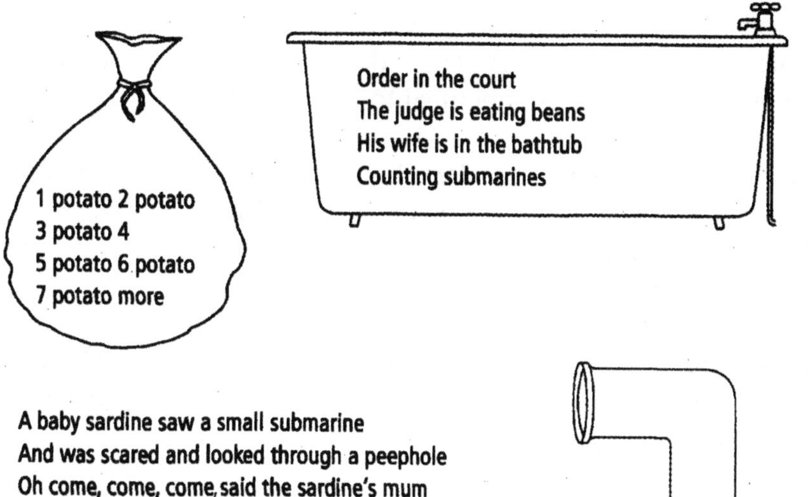

A baby sardine saw a small submarine
And was scared and looked through a peephole
Oh come, come, come, said the sardine's mum
It's only a tin full of people

The king or queen's rhythm

Have a crown to pass around: each child in turn is the king or queen and chooses an action. (At first have these ready – bowing, clapping, waving, curtsying, marching, saluting, then the children can add some more.) All do the action in time/in the rhythm of the word – bowing, bowing, bowing or saluting, saluting, saluting.

- Sing and use tuned instruments for pitch work to help develop the high and low tones of talk, the music of talk (prosody).
- Include some tapping out of syllables in your music or literacy sessions, this helps with spelling as well. Tap the children's names. Multi-syllabic words can be tapped out too; these can be curriculum vocabulary that also helps with this learning. Use picture references and, at first, mark the number of syllables.

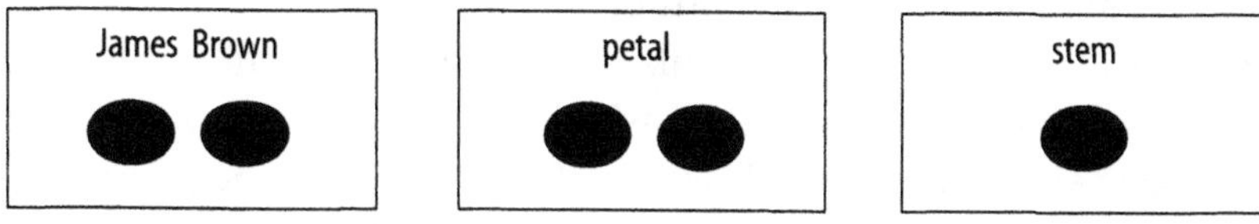

- Learn some rhymes/poems connected with curriculum areas that include particular sounds (see Appendix 3).

Vocabulary

Some children need support to acquire and use even common vocabulary and language concepts, and many older pupils still need concrete experiences to grasp new vocabulary.

2

Use a full multi-sensory approach wherever possible and consider the levels and ways of learning when planning how to help children learn and understand vocabulary. Use real or replica items wherever possible, so the children can handle them, look at them, hear them, talk about them in as many ways as possible. When this is not possible, photos or clear pictures are the next best. Follow-up writing and reading tasks can be structured to include specific vocabulary.

- Consider the key vocabulary that your pupils need to know in each subject area (see Appendix 2). Be realistic about what they will be able to learn or they may well 'switch off' and learn very little or nothing at all.
- Teach vocabulary words before presenting them in lessons. As part of this, teach them how to answer questions (Appendix 4). When the children are answering or asking questions, give them 'think about' prompts:

  What category does it belong to?
  What is it made from?
  What does it go with (brush with hair/teeth/dustpan)?
  Where could it be seen?
  Who made it/uses it?
  What does it sound/smell/feel/look like?
  Is it the name of something, describing something or about doing something (noun/adjective/verb)?
  What sound does it start/end with, what does it rhyme with, how many syllables has it got?

- Plan short but frequent practice times for this vocabulary. For instance, sing or chant the days of the week, the months of the year and the countries of Great Britain regularly during register/carpet time.
- Discuss familiar words when they are presented in new contexts, (light = not dark, light = not heavy).
- Instead of allowing free choice writing, ask for a piece about things that are rough and smooth, hot and cold, old and young, etc.
- Many concepts can be explored during science activities – wet/dry, hard/soft, rough/smooth etc.
- Consider a particular vocabulary list to work on with each class topic, and let parents know what it is so you can work on it together. If they are made aware of it, parents can help at home by mentioning and practising target vocabulary in everyday situations.
- Have a word or words of the week.
- Practise using imagery and 'thinking' pictures. Tell a short story, then show the children a picture or a set of pictures that illustrate this, then hide the picture(s) and tell the story again asking them to think the pictures. As they become more confident ask them to think their own pictures and tell the group about these. They can be encouraged to 'think pictures' while reading or tackling comprehension tasks.

'My mum took me.'
'Mmm, took you where?
'Yes.'
'Where did you go?'
'Yes, I went and it was so good.'

'He's very sizes.'
(He's very tall.)

- Older children may find it helpful to draw up charts or mind maps of key vocabulary, which can be added to and then used for reference. They could use a vocabulary reference book with their own terms and, alongside them, a choice of alternatives, e.g. sadness (sorrow, despair, gloom); happy (joyful, cheerful, ecstatic).
- **Vocabulary.** Older pupils need to explore additional vocabulary through use of antonyms, synonyms, root words, categorizations, associations and multiple meanings.
- Use commercial games and adapt others to learn and extend vocabulary. LDA has a range of interactive vocabulary and grammar activities on CD-ROM and Black Sheep Press has a range of reasonably priced, photocopiable materials. **Descriptive games** can be played with a range of pictures carefully selected to meet current language targets. There are commercial sets available, but newspapers, comics or wrapping paper are rich sources.
- **Four facts**. Have four counters and a set of model animals or pile of animal pictures in the middle. Each child in turn takes an animal and names it, then tries to give four facts/sentences about it. As they do so, put down a counter for each fact. When they have given four facts ask the rest of the group what else they know about the animal.
- **Verb game**. Have verbs written out on cards and practise performing these. After enough practice one pupil can perform a verb for the others to guess. It may be necessary to have a selection of the verbs on display at first so that the players can guess from this, rather than from memory. An adverb game can be played in the same way.

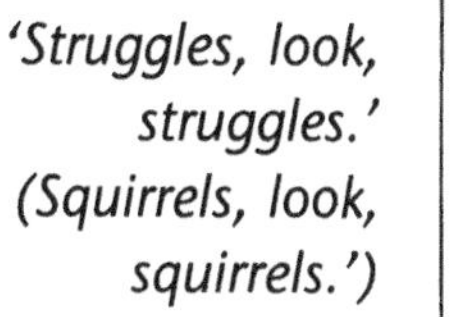
'Struggles, look, struggles.'
(Squirrels, look, squirrels.')

- **Guess the animal**. Have a set of animals hidden from general group view. Each child in turn comes out to choose an animal, keeping it hidden. Either have the child describe the animal for the others to guess or have the children ask questions to work out what the animal is. This game can be used for any vocabulary.

2

- **Word association**. Take a class word such as 'family' and collect as many words as possible for that family – baby, mum, dad, brother, aunt ...
- **Word association 2**. Take a word, perhaps from the current topic, and using prompts find as many other associated words as possible, e.g. wood:
  Family/category – plants or growing things.
  Function/what does it do, what do we do, who does this – provides home for animals, looks good, gives us wood to make things.
  Place or time – wood, garden, forest ...
  Appearance/parts, look, sound, smell, texture, size, shape – trunk, branches, leaves or rough bark, green leaves ...
  Reaction/how do you feel about it ...
- **Pairs**. Have pairs of cards with one on view or one of each in a pile from which the children select in turn and have to give the pair. Table and ... Cup and ... Postman and ...
- **20 questions**. Play this first with the items to be guessed in full view. As the children become more confident it can be tried with the items hidden or just thought of.
  Start at an easy level – 'I'm thinking of something grey with four legs' – and progress to – 'I'm thinking of something, it's animal' – and 20 questions are allowed in which to guess it. This helps develop questioning skills and can also be linked to current topic work. The definitions of the four possible categories of animal, vegetable, mineral and abstract would need to be discussed first. Older pupils may enjoy a simplified/customized version of Taboo or may be able to play the game itself.
- **Oral games**. Differentiation of work needs to include consideration of difficulties with literal interpretations, double meanings, colloquialisms, embedded clauses and other complex structures. Use or adapt oral games to target these. Try including one or two common expressions or sayings in each bank of topic work or linked to what you say in class, e.g. 'soft as butter/hard as nails' or 'pull your socks up'. These can be discussed, demonstrated and illustrated. (A useful booklet called 'Figures of speech' is available from AFASIC. We have also found these useful: *A Bird in the Hand* by Nigel Snell, published by Hamish Hamilton (1986, ISBN 0 241 11815 8), *Quick as a Cricket* by Audrey Wood, published by Child's Play (1982, ISBN 0 85953 306 9) and *120 Idioms at your fingertips* by June Nicols, published by STASS (ISBN 1 874534 9).

'Ben toilet gone.' (Ben has gone to the toilet.)

Grammar

There are various elements of grammar that cause problems for some children. Most of these need direct attention and would be included in the therapist's programme but also need to be included in class work.

Positional prepositions

(In, on, under, behind, in front, next to, across, against, far, near, etc.)

Some children need a lot of practice at these.

2

- They can be targeted directly in PE warm-up sessions, mathematics activities or geography activities when pupils can move behind, in front, over or under, or position apparatus.
- For younger children it is helpful to have a bag of items and containers to manipulate; puppets can be used too. The children can be directed to 'put the dog in the car', etc.
- Older children need to be exploring the wider and less obvious meanings of these positional words, e.g. **in** a box, **in** the garden, **in** a fix, **in** a muddle, **in** a mood, etc.

'I wented to the swimming.'

'You went to the swimming pool, and what did you do there?'

'I am swimming now and she is splashing me but I do not like that.'

Personal pronouns

Many children with speech and language difficulties muddle these. 'Me' is used when it should be 'I'; Mr, Mrs, Aunt and Uncle, etc. will cause problems as well as she/he and her/him, etc. They can be practised in context at home and at school and pointed out in reading, writing and speaking activities.

- Each child can carry out an action, or mime an occupation for the others to guess using he/she.
- A commentary on a video or description of a picture can be given using target pronouns.
- Photographs of a child's extended family or a fictitious family can be used to target family words such as aunt/uncle, cousin, brother/sister.
- Multiple mime: this is one of our made-up games where the group mimes a chosen job or action in a range of ways with appropriate individual and group commentary. So one girl mimes and says, **'I** am cooking', then the group chorus, **'She** is cooking'. One boy mimes for **I** am cooking/**He** is cooking. Several children for **We** are cooking/**They** are cooking and everyone for **We** are cooking. We have added **My** meal is delicious/**Our** meal is delicious/**Their** meal is delicious and included associated phrases to practise his/her/mine/ours.

  It is helpful to have picture reference clues in sight at first. We have adapted this to practise adjectives, adverbs, position words and a range of targeted vocabulary in conjunction with pronouns. In this way we can revisit areas of language again and again, which is just what our children need. Older pupils could play it as a guessing game.
- Change the words of well-known songs to practise he/she or other personal pronouns e.g:

'Megan put the kettle on, **she** will put the kettle on, **she** will put the kettle on, **we**'ll all have tea.
James take it off again, **he** will take it off again, **he** will take it off again, **we**'ll all go away.

- **His/hers** or **him/her** can be practised with a set of objects: each child chooses one and places it in front of themselves. Go round the circle chanting, 'The blue pencil is **his**', 'The red pencil is **hers**', about the items.
  Or 'The blue pencil is by **him**', 'The red pencil is by **her**'.
  Or, Teacher: 'Andy what do you want?' Andy says he wants the blue pencil so the teacher says, 'Andy wants the blue pencil, give it to **him**'. The child with the blue pencil hands it over then says, 'I've given it to **him**'.
- Have a large picture of a girl and a boy and assorted clothes, etc. If you use sticky-backed Velcro it will work better. Each child in turn places an item on either the girl or the boy, you can colour code if you wish to guide the choice. The player can say, 'This is **his/hers**' or 'This belongs to **him/her**', or any sentence pattern that includes the target words.

Or use the children in the group and their features and belongings.
Winslow has a new Pronoun Party Game Board pack that has eight games and which our children really like.

Plurals

The children may miss these out in speaking, reading and writing. These can be practised in context as above and pointed out and taught in literacy work.

- Make up a set of picture cards to illustrate different plurals: newspapers and magazines are good sources. We have a set that our younger children really like that includes one cat up one tree, two cats up one tree, two cats up two trees and one cat up two trees and other amusing combinations.
- There are plurals games produced by LDA, among other organizations.
- Use some of the miming games above to target plurals.

- Point out plurals in number rhymes, stories, etc. Then follow up with a game of plurals. Give a word or a sentence, depending on the level at which you're working and the children have to make it a plural. As they become more confident the children can also take a turn at giving the singular starting point, or the plural could be given to be made into the singular.

2

Tenses

- Use pictures or the job titles of a range of occupations, such as teacher, doctor, plumber, etc. Each child in turn can mime an occupation for the others to guess. It may be helpful to practise the mimes as a group first. This can be extended to the group or individual players giving a description of a task relating to the work of an occupation using past, present and future tenses (the doctor took/is taking/will take the patient's temperature).
- Set up a daily calendar that can provide a short but regular exercise in using simple past, present and future tenses to describe personal activities. Send a simple photocopiable calendar home so parents can join in. This will also reassure and support those children who wake up not knowing what day it is nor what is likely to happen on any given day (see Appendix 6).
- Use art, design and cookery activities for memory and recall but also structure them to practise using past, present and future tenses. Practise tenses in prediction and retelling work during reading activities.
- Use picture sequences for storytelling of what has happened, is happening and will happen next. This can be extended into story writing and, as pupils become more confident, only give the past and present, asking the pupils to put in their own ideas for the future/what will happen next.
- Passive structures need particular attention: 'The cat was chased by the mouse' is the type of sentence that trips up some pupils. It may be helpful to give or get the pupils to draw a pictorial representation; these could be literal, taken from current classwork texts or fantasy (which are great fun). A set of such pictures could then be used as a 'guess the sentence' game or a game where the pupils have to ask the group questions about the drawing. Later the written sentences can be used on their own.

  Amy was following Ben.
  Jack was chased by the giant.
  The princess was caught by the dragon.

'Him not know him not.' (Said in disgust about his female teacher.)

Omissions

Some children miss out words and word parts that have less stress within a phrase or sentence, such as: **a**, **and**, **the**, **ing**, **ed**, plural **s**. They may do this when speaking, reading and writing.

2

- If a child is persistently missing them out in his own writing 'Breakthrough to Literacy'-type folders can be useful. Older children can be taught to look through personal writing to check if all the appropriate words and word parts on a reference chart have been included.
- Children can use a highlighter pen and look for them in given passages. Newspaper articles are useful for this.
- They can be built into or pointed out in reading and writing tasks.
- It can also be helpful to practise tapping out the number of words in given sentences or those taken from the child's writing.

Sentences and non-sentences

- Give and identify sentences and non-sentences about the children in the group:
  Jane has brown hair - sentence.
  Jane brown hair - non-sentence.
  Then give some more, one at a time, and ask children to call out sentence or non-sentence.
  As they become familiar with this, use objects and/or pictures to give sentences and non-sentences.
- Words in a sentence. Write down simple, monosyllabic word sentences about the children (if a child has a multi-syllabic name at first use he/she) and show them how many words are in each sentence. Show them how to put out one counter for each word, then clap the words while saying the sentence (He has brown hair - four counters). As they become familiar with this, go on to include multi-syllabic words (Amanda has long eyelashes - eight counters). Progress to saying a sentence where they put out counters for each word, rather than show it and say it.

Am an da has long eye lash es

● ● ● ● ● ● ● ●

Then you can add an agreed sign/symbol for a full stop to be put at the end of each sentence and some way of indicating the capital letter - try raising hands high and saying capital and knocking on the floor while saying full stop.

3 Receptive Language

Children with receptive difficulties have problems understanding even common language and may have difficulty knowing when language is directed at, or pertinent to, them. They may avoid eye contact, avoid situations that they find difficult, or avoid speech – this may give the appearance of a hearing loss, so deep is the level of 'shutting off' in some children.

'How are you?'
'I'm seven.'

Avoidance, when you think about it, is a logical step to take. Since they cannot make sense of the language around them and easily become 'overloaded' with language, they shut it all out. Alternatively, they may be concentrating too hard on one word or phrase and trying to make sense of it – so that they shut out the rest.

They may look blank, pull faces, smile or giggle, cry or sulk, hide or hit out. They may carry on doing the same thing although you think you've clearly told them to stop, or they may do the opposite of what you say, or smile and nod – then do nothing. They may respond inappropriately because they misunderstand. They may echo or endlessly repeat what you have said, in their search for meaning.

Older children will be expected to deal successfully with more and more complex language; it may not always be apparent that they are having difficulty, or which particular structure or item of vocabulary they don't understand. As they get older, they are less willing to ask for help and they learn to disguise their difficulties.

'How are you?'
'I'm Nick.'

In a busy classroom, children with receptive difficulties can easily be overlooked. They may quickly acquire a range of strategies to compensate for their lack of understanding. They may shadow another child who is in the same group and copy what she/he does. They may frequently visit the toilet, lose their books or equipment. They may have a lot of headaches or stomach-aches. They may change the subject and talk excessively about something that they are sure of. Children can become so expert at these tactics that teachers and parents are unaware of what is going on.

Whether experiencing minor or severe difficulties, such children will need direct support to listen with understanding and to follow instructions.

Listening and understanding

Children with receptive difficulties have major problems with understanding and these can affect reading and writing, as well as spoken language. In all these areas, the language used needs to be simplified. Continually check for understanding and if you suspect a difficulty:

- Repeat, 'chunking' the language with pauses to allow time for each 'chunk' to be processed.
- Simplify and rephrase, taking out unnecessary words and explaining vocabulary.
- Ask the pupil to repeat back, in their own words, what has been said or what they are to do. In this way, understanding can be checked.
- Be ready to give more time for a child to process what has been said.

Child hits her own head and says, 'I can't get it, nothing is sense today.'

Teacher to child standing rigidly rooted to the spot, holding his breath: 'Are you all right?' 'I'm pulling myself together.'

3

Teachers should carefully consider the language of instruction they use in lessons, giving clear explanations and being ready to repeat and/or simplify as necessary. Use visual clues to support the oral input. Build this into overall planning and practise and extend key vocabulary as part of everyday lessons.

In addition:

- Consider the position of the children concerned. Seat them where your eye falls; this is not necessarily right by you. Make sure there is enough room during carpet time. Put them where there is the least distraction.
- Verbal messages are problematical so consider putting the main message last. Messages to go home should be given last thing in the day; get the child to repeat back and always give a written note when possible. (For older children messages can be put on the board for pupils to copy.)
- Older pupils need to learn and practise self-help strategies, such as acceptable ways of asking for an instruction to be repeated or to say that they have not understood. This may seem obvious but many pupils with SLI have particular difficulties with such pragmatic language skills.

'Dad was cutting the grass with a . . . grass scraper.'

Listening

Many children in mainstream and specialist settings need to develop good listening skills. There are a number of reasons why children do not seem to be good listeners.

Some children may have immature attention control and may be poor at switching from monitoring sounds to focused listening, when they need to listen for a purpose.

If we think of Reynell's stages of attention control some children of school age may still be at stage two.

Developmental language scales

Reynell, J. (1976) *Developmental Language Scales* NFER/Nelson

Stage 1: 0–1 year	Can pay fleeting attention but any new event will distract. Language interferes with attention.
Stage 2: 1–2 years	Will attend to own choice of activity, but will not tolerate intervention, particularly verbal. Attention is single channelled. Language interferes with attention. Must ignore other stimuli in order to concentrate on chosen activity.
Stage 3: 2–3 years	Still single channelled. Will attend to adults' choice of activity, but still difficult to control. Child must stop play to attend to adults. Must listen and then shift attention back to activity with adult help.
Stage 4: 3–4 years	Single channelled, but more easily controlled. Adult verbalization of tasks helps. Can shift attention between task and adult.
Stage 5: 4–5 years	Normal school entrant. Integrated attention for short spell. Attention span is still short. Child listens to instructions without interrupting activity to look at speaker. Child externalizes language.
Stage 6: 5–6 years	Mature school entrant. Integrated attention is well controlled and sustained. Child internalizes language.

Also consider that previous experiences of listening may not match school expectations.

Language at home	**Language at school**
Mainly conversation about the 'here and now' or about shared experiences, events and people. Not as much inferential thinking required.	Not so often about the 'here and now', more often about the past or the future and may be about new events and people. These are more likely not to be experienced at first hand. Inferential thinking required.
Tends to be more casual, with each person contributing when they have something to share or to ask.	More formalized: discussion, question and answer, following instructions.
Talking takes place in a smaller group, children getting more individual and more immediate feedback.	Takes place in a larger group, children have to take and wait their turn, less immediate feedback.
Talking takes place in a smaller group, children getting more individual and more immediate feedback.	Group identity may be poor. More likely to be group directions or questions, some children may not realize this is directed at them as part of the group.
Homes are busy and noisy places and some children may not have developed focused listening.	Schools are busy and noisy – often this is connected to activity, children are expected to listen through the noise.
Quiet may alarm them or may be linked directly with bed and sleep time, i.e. time for not listening.	Children are expected to be quiet at times so that they can listen. Conversely, some children may think that being quiet is enough and may not be engaging in active listening.
May be supported by visual clues such as television, enabling the listener to pick up on information that he/she has not necessarily heard or understood. Some children may have become over-reliant on visual clues.	Not always supported visually.
At home 'Listen' does not always mean that you have to listen first time, as instructions may be repeated or allowances made.	Time is precious and there's lots to do so in school pupils are expected to listen well the first time.
Comparatively short listening sessions, many of which do not require a response – TV, parents' commentary.	Extended listening that usually requires a response.
May not understand what 'Listen' means but within the family allowances can be made.	In school we expect children to know what 'Listen' means. Some children need to be directly taught the sub-skills of good listening and need time and support to practise and develop these.

The following Involvement scale, taken from an article by Chris Rider 'Well-being and involvement' in *Special Children* (Feb./Mar. 2002), is also extremely useful (reproduced with permission from Questions Publishing).

Involvement Scale

Involvement Scale
Level 1 • Frequently non-active • Absent-minded/aimless • Not really aware of what they are doing, not purposefully active • Appears to be involved but actions are stereotypical/repetitive
Level 2 • Sporadic activity • Occasionally doing puzzles, playing in water ... • Daydreaming and messing around/dabbling
Level 3 • Usually engaged in some sort of activity • Activity lacks intensity • Performance is a succession of meaningless actions • Aware of own actions • Lack of energy • Often easily distracted • Short attention span
Level 4 • Usually active • Activity has real meaning • Operates near boundaries of capacity • May need some support or stimulation
Level 5 • Often shows involvement in activities • Continuously engaged in meaningful activities • Easily makes choices • Not easily distracted • Involvement is natural – not through strength of will • Intrinsic motivation • Persistence, energy, complexity are generally present

There may also be other physical, emotional or neurological difficulties:

- Hearing problems including 'Glue ear' and fluctuating hearing loss caused by hay fever, colds, etc.
- Auditory processing difficulties – difficulty perceiving and processing language. Children may have difficulty picking out from background noise or a lot of information what is relevant or pertinent to them.
- Memory difficulties.
- SLI mild or moderate.
- Have seen, seeing, waiting to see speech therapist.
- Anxiety or stress.
- ADHD.

3

Time spent on establishing the methods and rules for good listening within class will benefit the whole class and if a whole-school approach is taken it will benefit everyone. Such activities can be included directly as part of National Curriculum work in English (speaking and listening), music and RE or PSHE and in all subject areas as part of effective class management.

First talk about what constitutes good listening, why it is necessary and how practice can improve memory and recall. Good listening helps us to:

- learn well
- make friends and be a good friend.

3

Good listening can be broken down into several sub-skills:

- Good sitting – still, quiet, not fidgeting, where you can see the person who is talking.
- Good looking – at the person who is talking.
- Good thinking – listening to what is said, thinking about what is said, perhaps making a picture in your head. If it is an instruction then maybe the child needs to whisper the key words to himself until he can visualize them or think them inside his own head. (It may be necessary to describe this process to the child.)
- Taking turns – knowing when it is your turn and waiting your turn – using conversational devices such as nodding, saying 'mmmm' or 'OK'.

Teacher putting papers on one side, 'I don't think I'll need these yet.' Later, she finds that Child A has put them in the bin, thinking that the teacher didn't need them at all.

It is useful to include these in a whole-school policy and have picture references on view in each class. These rules can be established as part of the code of conduct, and referred to and practised when necessary. It is helpful to some children (and good fun) to act out good sitting/bad sitting, etc.

It is also helpful to flag up focused listening times so that those who have difficulty switching between monitoring and focused listening are given an extra cue. They may also need to be addressed by name and to be shown a visual prompt. It may be helpful to briefly point out what they have to be listening for in the ensuing input, using a list or pictograms/pictures as a reminder.

Older children still need to be reminded of these but may handle the points better if they are written in a more age-appropriate way:

- Sit well (good posture, good position).
- Look regularly at the person who is talking.
- Be attentive, listen and indicate that you are listening by nodding or affirming (uh-huh, yes, no, mmmm). Make a mental picture of key points as someone is talking. Figure out the key points to note down. Unobtrusive note-taking (Note-taking is a skill that may need specific teaching and practice.)

- Maintain the flow of conversation/discussion by taking turns and if you wish to interrupt use an acceptable method ('Ah but, just let me say at this point . . .' 'I need to tell you this now before I forget.')

It is helpful to discuss good listening in different contexts, such as church, canteen, yard, etc., and useful to involve parents of children with speech and language difficulties since they will be able to establish good listening in home contexts.

3

Memory

There are different kinds of memory problems but, whatever kind of problem is involved, it is important that the child concerned is given time in a supportive and calm atmosphere. Acknowledge the situation and explain that many grown-ups have this problem too. Discuss the strategies below and select one to try. If it's not helping try another. This kind of approach is less likely to cause panic, or a feeling of defeat or failure, and may just trigger the memory and allow the child to contribute.

Word finding

Some children have particular difficulty recalling words and need help to develop strategies to overcome this problem. We have probably all experienced this at some time, when a word is 'on the tip of our tongue' but we just can't recall it and the harder we try, the less likely it is that we will. Children with word-finding difficulties experience this frequently. The aim is for each child to find a strategy that works and to become adept at using it independently. Try:

After intensive work on 'rough/smooth' – 'Remember we're thinking about rough and smooth.' R, picking up cheese grater and feeling it carefully, 'Yes, it's hard.'

- prompting with the first sound;
- prompting with a description of the object's size, shape, colour;
- giving the opposite: it's not black it's **** (white);
- giving something similar: it's like a mouse, it's a g**** (gerbil).

Sometimes it is difficult to use any of these if you have little idea of the word the child is trying to recall.

Generally, much vocabulary work is needed. The children need to increase their vocabulary and descriptive abilities through direct labelling of objects, pictures and characters.

They need to practise various ways of defining words:

- **Category**: orange – fruit
  bus – vehicle
  pen – tool

- **Function**:
  orange – to be eaten
  bus – to ride on, to go on a journey on
  pen – to write with
- **Characteristics**:
  orange – orange, spherical or round
  bus – lots of wheels, lots of windows, lots of seats, upstairs and downstairs, tickets
  pen – ink, nib
- **Location**:
  orange – fruit bowl, fruit shop, supermarket, sandwich box, tree in hot country
  bus – road, school, bus station
  pen – school, pencil case, shop
- **Synonym**:
  orange – tangerine
  bus – coach
  pen – biro

'Greg, will you please pass me a black felt pen and a ruler.' Greg listens carefully but passes only a ruler.

3

Encourage and praise any attempt made to get meaning across. It doesn't matter what words are used, e.g. 'You know, the place where we eat dinner.' 'Oh yes, you mean the hall.' Then play some word games with school vocabulary including the word 'hall'. Later check if this word has been remembered.

- Play a game using some of the ideas given above. Start with objects in sight. 'I'm thinking of something in the classroom. It's brown, plastic and has four legs – you sit on a . . .' Then let the child have a turn at describing for others to guess.
- Use incomplete sentences – we cut with . . ., we write with . . .
- Use pairs – cup and . . ., paper and . . .
- Use word association. Collect as many words as possible for one given word or category – **family** – mum, dad, gran, brother, sister, etc. This is a useful strategy to use at the start of a new topic in any curriculum subject to gauge what vocabulary is known. It can then be used at the end of this topic to see what vocabulary has been learned and remembered.

Short-term auditory memory

- First practise instant recall so that what is said by the leader is instantly repeated back. This can be done with instructions in class, which will have been 'chunked' for ease of understanding. It can be done for a very short time each day as an individual, paired or class activity. It can be done in the way you dismiss a class or get a class to line up. It can be done at home, or in the car if parents are involved.
- Use a child's strengths, so, if a child is musical, sing a list, or if a child has good visual skills let him read the list, in words or pictures, first.

G had lost his favourite scarf. 'Mrs M, I can't find my neck wrapper.'

- Many children with speech and language difficulties find delivering messages problematical. This can first be practised as an instant activity within class as a sort of 'Chinese whispers' game.
  It can then be structured so that a child practises the message but has a written back-up with him. In this way useful techniques such as mnemonics and visual imagery can be developed.
- Use some of the games below as a warm up in PE, in music sessions, in circle time, in PSHE, in literacy or in any curriculum subject wherever appropriate.

Short-term visual memory

Use the same principles of little and often at first. If trying to establish a sight vocabulary, for instance, have the child look at the target words for a short time every day. It is often most productive to use a multi-sensory approach and look while finger tracing a few times, then with eyes closed write/draw in the air or on a rough, carpeted surface. This can be a pre-cursor to a look, say, cover, write/draw, check technique. Some games/activities below are specifically to develop visual memory.

Long-term auditory and visual memory

In many of the games below it is possible to introduce a time delay by counting to five or ten before the child can carry out the activity. This is one way of making the task harder and lengthening the recall time. This should be done gradually, and written or pictorial back-ups provided as prompts at first to boost confidence. Other ways to make the games more challenging include increasing the number of items used, stipulating a certain order of recall and introducing a distraction.

- It is a useful exercise to learn rhymes and poems (Appendix 3).
- Give a word at register time to be remembered, at first until break, or lunchtime, then all day.

The child should have regular turns at giving instructions to the others, including the adult.

- Try mnemonics with older children. If shopping for cake, apples and toothpaste the initials of the three items can be put into the word CAT (I do this all the time to remember things!). Try visual imagery - picture yourself eating a cake and an apple, then brushing your teeth. Offer different strategies to a child but help him find the one that works for him, that he can use independently. Mnemonics will not work for some children with severe and persistent memory difficulties.

Accept that there will be some children who will need to carry prompts, filofaxes or use charts and lists of key facts and vocabulary for a considerable time. Teach the use of these aids as early as possible so that they become normal practice. Clear plastic wallets, such as those used for carrying store and credit cards, can be purchased cheaply. These can be used as personal memory files and can be carried around easily by pupils and be therefore readily available for reference and for revision. They can be customized for each pupil including prompts and reminders as well as information, e.g. words and facts that they are trying to remember. Teach the use of these aids as early as possible so that it becomes normal practice. Show pupils the need for regular revision to facilitate information being stored in long-term memory. The Ebbinghaus diagram shows this clearly.

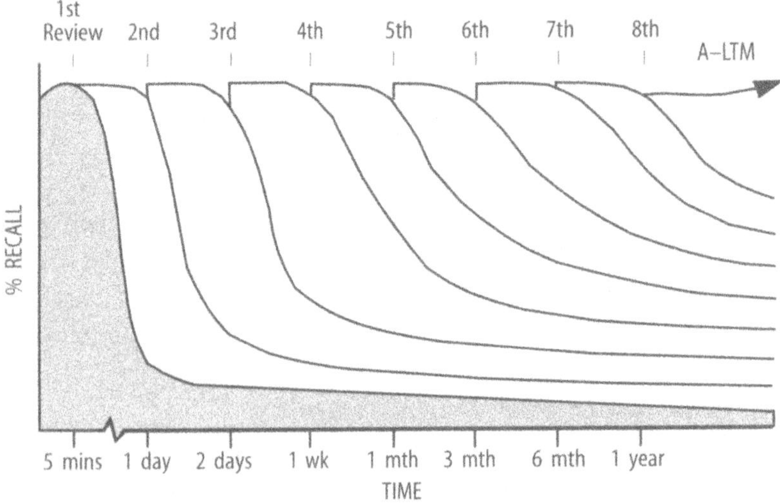

If it is not reviewed only 20% of new or unfamiliar information is remembered the next day

Effect on recall of a properly planned revision programme
Ebbinghaus, H. (1964) in *Memory: A Contribution to Experimental Psychology*

Listening and memory games and activities

All the vocabulary and grammar games and activities given earlier can also be used to check understanding and to develop listening skills.

- Giving instructions and following instructions can be built into lessons as an introduction or a short activity, e.g. music (how to play), geography (directions), PE (directions for warm-up), English (speaking and listening) or IT (roamer activities).
- Allocate five or ten minutes regularly to giving instructions in class. This can be done each time children line up to leave the class, e.g. 'Children with long hair line up', 'Children with laces go and wash hands', 'Children with short hair stand on one leg'.
- Giving instructions. Have a leader give several instructions. The players have to listen and carry them out in order when the leader has finished speaking. Encourage the children to say the key points out loud at first, then to whisper them, then to say them silently inside their heads. Start with short, easy ones (hop to the door) and gradually increase the length. Give simple instructions. These will have to be tailored to the level of the

group but can include colours/numbers of things or times to do an action/position/curriculum/vocabulary/class equipment/ clothes/people.

For example:

- Touch something red then stand behind your chair.
- Clap two times then stand near a door.
- Point to something made of metal then stand in front of your chair.
- Hold up a ruler then put it under the table.
- If you are wearing white socks jump three times.
- Touch something made of wood then stand by a grown-up.
- Hop to the window and crawl back to your chair.
- Before you sit down clap twice.
  (NB there is a progression with before/after instructions:
  Clap your hands before you sit down (order of presentation).
  After you sit down clap your hands (order of presentation).
  Before you sit down clap your hands (not order of presentation).
  Clap your hands after you sit down (not order of presentation).
- Don't touch red, touch blue.
- Everyone except the children with laces stand up.
- In pairs or groups children take it in turns to give instructions for building with Lego, using multi-link, using calculators, etc.
- **Listen to the percussion instruments**. Have two sets of percussion instruments, one set in sight and one set hidden. Children close their eyes while you play one, then open their eyes and put a hand up if they can identify and play the instrument. Now send one child to the hidden set to play an instrument while the others listen and then identify and play the target instrument. The difficulty can be increased by playing two instruments and then three, and by the children having to play the instruments in the right order.
- **Sabotage.** Set up obstacles to understanding to teach pupils that there will be times when they have to ask for clarification. Hide coats or pencils so that the children have to seek help. Have a colleague or another pupil make a noise/distraction while you are talking. Deliberately use words beyond that pupil's understanding. Cough or mumble part-way through talking. Of course it goes without saying that it should be explained to pupils before starting, treated as a game and appropriate encouragement and rewards given. Maggie Johnson gives more ideas on this in her booklet 'Active Listening'.
- **Give simple instructions.** (Simon Says) Let the children have three lives, then play as 'ghosts' if they lose all of them. Start by giving the Simon Says actions in a level tone and demonstrating them, giving the other - non-Simon Says instructions - in a different, higher tone and not doing them. As the children improve, don't demonstrate the actions. Then as they improve further, use a level tone throughout.

- **Odd one out. Minimal pairs**. Listen and tell the difference between minimal pair words, e.g. **Man/Can Man/Map Man/Men**. Initially it is probably best to use a selection that differ by first letter, then some that differ by the last letter, then by the middle letter, then a random set.
- **What's missing?** Read a list with one thing missing – days of the week, numbers, well-known rhyme, etc.
- **Listen for the word that starts with a different sound:**

apple	ant	egg	animal
boat	bat	ball	skates
car	my	coat	cow
dog	five	ditch	dad
egg	envelope	elephant	ink
fire	far	candy	feather

  And so on. Later, lists with one different final sound or vowel sound can be used.
- **Word/digit repeat**. Listen and repeat back words, sentences or numbers. Start with two, and when pupils are generally good at remembering those, move on:

  apple, orange, red, yellow, blue
  dog, cat, mouse, gerbil

  (4,6) (1,3,5) (2,6,10,4)

  I climbed.
  He is tired.
  She went to school.
  He climbed up to the top.
- **Remember and reverse**
  As the pupil becomes good at remembering and repeating back numbers or words try the same activity but this time the numbers or words have to be repeated back in reverse order; this is exercising the working memory. For example, say to the pupil '7, 2', he has to repeat back '2, 7'; or say 'The man is big' and he has to repeat back 'big is man the'.
- **Fruit salad**. Give each child round the circle the name of a fruit (colour or vehicle or animal) in sets of three – apple, banana, orange, apple, banana, orange and so on round the circle. (If you have a larger group adjust the number of names accordingly – have five or six – apple, orange, banana, lemon, pear, grape.)

  Establish rules – walking carefully, no bumping, into middle and out to a different place. Then play the game where the ones you call swap places, so if you call 'apples, oranges' they swap and if you call 'bananas, oranges' they swap and if you call 'fruit salad' everybody swaps.
- **Using a calculator**. Ask the children to key in numbers; start with two and work up to five or six. Say the numbers for the children to remember. They enter them, then show you the numbers.

- **Multi-link.** The children have their hands in their laps while you say two colours (start with two and work up to five or six). The children remember and pick up the colours and hide them in their hands until everyone's done, then you check. When they've got used to the routine they can take turns choosing/giving colours.
  Each child has 10 multi-link, one of each colour.
  Join a red one and a blue one.
  Join red, blue, green.
  Join all except the blue and green ...
  Give each child a multi-link cube; some can have the same colours.
  Reds stand.
  Reds and greens change places.
  Reds and blues stand; greens and yellows lie down.
  If you have red clap twice ...
- **Giving clues.** The children take it in turns to give three clues about a picture while the others listen and decide what it is. To check for good listening ask children at the end what clues have been given. The use of pictures keeps children on track and ensures that they don't change their minds halfway through.
- **Pairs.** Working in pairs, the children ask each other about a given subject and then report back to the group (their partner's favourite food, drink, colour, number, game, TV programme, pets, brother's and sister's names ...).
- **Listen for a category**. The children have to repeatedly stand up or sit down as they hear a word from a given category. Name the category then read in a level voice, or tape-record and play back while joining in or observing. It is easier with two adults, one to read in a level tone and the other to monitor what the children do. So if the named category is 'food', the children stand, sit, stand, and sit as they hear each food word. (If preferred the children can raise and lower their arms instead.) For example, red, **apple**, skirt, one, cat, knife, green, **toast**, horse, mum, nine, **baked beans**, etc.
- **Say and ask**. Tell the children what category they are listening for – vehicles, for example. Read each group of four then ask, 'What vehicles did I say?'

  NB Use the list this way first so the target words are the last ones. Then try reversing the list so the target words are said first and have to be remembered longer.

apple	banana	car	bus
orange	yellow	lorry	train
elephant	giraffe	boat	hovercraft
four	five	bike	plane

  Use lists of words that begin with the same sound, category lists, vocabulary lists, linked to particular subject areas, random numbers.

3

3

Tell a simple one or two sentence 'story' and ask a question about it. As children become familiar with this lengthen the sentences and/or ask more questions or make them inferential.

A boy called Tom went to the park and played on the swing.
Who went to the park? What did he play on?
I went to Chester on the bus.
Where did I go? How did I get there?
I had my tea at Carol's house.
Where did I eat? What meal did I have?
The next day my sister and I went to town.
When did they go? Where did they go? Who went to town?
My sister said, 'I'm helping Mum to clear up.'
Who is helping Mum? What are they doing? Who is speaking?

- **Describe one child in minute detail**. Child concerned stands up if they think it's them; others put their hands up if they know who it is. (NB Children need to become aware when they have been given enough information to make a good guess.)
  I'm thinking of someone who has white socks.
  I'm thinking of someone who has white socks and blue eyes.
  I'm thinking of someone who has white socks, blue eyes and brown hair.
  I'm thinking of someone who has white socks, blue eyes and long, brown hair.
- **Listening and drawing, circling, colouring** ...
  Photocopiable sheets and on cassette (see resources list).
- **Whisper game.** Have children close their eyes or sit round with you in the middle. Whisper their names for them to line up at the door ready to move on. If they get good at this make it harder – whisper initials or descriptions or simply look directly at each child in turn to signal that they are to line up.
- **Kim's game.** A number of items are placed on a tray or table. Choose a set pertinent to current work, e.g. fabric, glass, wood, metal, plastic items when covering 'materials'. The child or children are given a chance to look at them, then they turn away and close their eyes.

One item is removed and this has to be named after a second look at the tray. The number of items removed can gradually be increased. Or use a magazine picture that has lots of detail, look at it then cover it and try to remember as many items as you can.

- **Traffic police.** Make up some car number plates on paper or card. One player is the robber who moves a number across the table; the policeman has to look carefully at it. The robber hides the number and the policeman has to write it down or radio it to headquarters.

- **Jigsaws.** Teach the child a system, so he is looking for pieces that fit together by colour, shape, parts of objects and edge and middle pieces. Then try to complete it using shape alone, by turning the jigsaw over onto its plain, reverse side.

3

Supportive signing

It may be helpful to consider using a supportive signing system that runs alongside spoken language. Communication is obviously difficult for our children, whether they have a severe speech production difficulty, a receptive difficulty or an expressive difficulty. But many children have well-developed visual skills and respond well to staff using mime and gesture. Paget Gorman Signed Speech (PGSS) has been specifically designed for use with children with speech and language impairment. It is not a language in its own right but accompanies talk. Paget is a very logical system based on a number of hand shapes and basic signs that are linked to class groups, such as animals, vehicles, food, etc. It is also possible to sign all grammatical markers such as plurals, tense endings, possessives, etc. It can be used to:

- introduce and support the acquisition of specific vocabulary and language concepts;
- introduce and support the acquisition of specific grammatical terms;
- encourage children to include all necessary words in an utterance;
- slow down speech in children who rush their talk and push all their words together;
- assist decoding during reading without verbally interrupting the reader.

In addition Cued Articulation, a signing system designed particularly to assist children with speech production, has proved extremely useful when working with children with speech production difficulties. It enables us to cue them into a particular sound in a

aeroplane

3

way that is low-key and yet reminds them how to shape their tongue and lips and how to form the sound. It can be used alongside such materials as Jolly Phonics.

Paget and Cued Articulation may not be suitable for all educational settings but it may be worthwhile exploring available systems and ways of visually cueing and supporting children with speech and language difficulties.

4 Social Use of Language Skills and Behaviour

'I think I'll tidy for you Mrs M.'
'It's playtime. Don't you want to go out and play?'
'Well you see I try to get their names cos I don't know their names and I say can I play, but they run away.'
'Mmmm what about joining a ring game or a game that you know, that has started?'
'Well you see if I go wrong they say, oh you, you can't play – and I can't really – so I feel all on myself, all on myself and I don't want to walk round again all on myself you see.'

The playground can be a frightening, lonely place.

Many children with speech and language impairment are unable to interpret their peers' colloquial language, jokes, nuances and implied meanings and this impedes the development of social relationships and making friends. They can be really lonely and ready targets for bullying, yet unable to use language to explain their predicament accurately or to resolve the conflict. They may use inappropriate behaviour if they have poor understanding of body language, gesture, greetings and acceptable forms of address.

Some of these difficulties are to do with what are termed 'pragmatic language skills'; these are bound up in the culture and customs of society, family and friends. They are the sorts of skills that are very hard to teach, and most of us learn them as we go along; for example, knowing that it is more acceptable to say 'Good morning' to a teacher rather than 'Hiya, how ya doin?' Or that while it is acceptable to say 'Good night' several times to the same people, initially when you go to bed, later when you come back down for the book you've forgotten and later still to get a drink ... in the morning you only say 'Good morning' once to each person.

Pupils with poor social language skills may be the pupils whose names are mentioned frequently in staffrooms, as teachers, other adults and peers may interpret their responses in a range of negative ways. Such pupils may:

- 'switch off' during lessons because they have very poor listening and understanding skills;
- be restless, fidgety and may shout out;
- have difficulty following instructions;
- appear unconcerned if they forget to bring things from home;
- answer rather strangely using the wrong words or a literal interpretation;
- be noticed a lot at playtimes because they are more 'physical' than other children;
- be socially immature and have co-ordination problems;
- have difficulties remembering names, following games, joining in with chatter;
- often be on their own or complaining that no one will play with them;
- seem to be 'saying and doing it on purpose'.

Younger children will need help to develop play skills; ring games have proved most useful and can be readily adapted. (There are a number of books that have a selection of playground games listed in the Books and Resources section.) In Acton Park Infants School we have a whole-school system that supports all children. We actively teach ring games and then reward children for playing these. Each child has a 100-square playground chart and at breaktimes duty staff give out stickers to be stuck on these charts. The children are rewarded in a weekly service for each set of ten stickers earned. This has worked well as all the children have knowledge of the same games and it is both easier for them to join and follow games and for staff to prompt and encourage good play. Incidentally, this system has also developed mathematics skills: all the children know how many stickers they have and their ability to count in tens quickly improves! In the summer, we use a range of equipment designed to be fun but also effective in developing motor skills as well as social skills (French skipping, large noughts and crosses, skipping ropes, target hoopla games). I have found it helpful to spend some additional time teaching my pupils the ring games and how to use the playtime equipment so they are more confident at playtimes.

Some children find peer group jargon and social situations especially difficult because they interpret language absolutely literally. This can be addressed directly by collecting, explaining and using common colloquial expressions and sayings; for example phrases used by adults such as 'Pull your socks up' and 'Jump to it'. These can be found in written materials and they can be directly linked to topic work. In addition, take note of those expressions in current vogue such as 'Wicked', 'Monstrous' or 'Cool'. Similarly, slightly older children can explore and collect different kinds of jokes and puns. It has proved useful for older children to learn to recognize such language for themselves. They can report statements that sound odd or nonsensical, discuss and possibly collect them for reference. A few years ago 'Well bad' was much in use in the playground – a trial for those children who literally interpret and for whom it didn't make sense.

Mr M used to tap his watch and say 'What time do you call this?' when a pupil was late. When Mr M himself was late G leapt to his feet, tapped his watch and said very loudly, 'What time do you call this?'

Flat speech, with no intonation and little or no expression, can also be a characteristic linked to difficulties with understanding and with being understood. Speaking with expression can be demonstrated in the activities above and can also be demonstrated and practised while reading and through role-play and drama. It has proved helpful to discuss and explore body language, ways of speaking with different expression, greetings and partings as discrete skills and then to practise these.

- **How are you feeling?** In my class we have a feelings board and each morning the children consider how they are feeling and put their name by the appropriate label – happy/sad/worried/full of beans/excited/tired. This provides a short opportunity to discuss why we have put our names by a particular label. We have now developed this to discussing some ways we can 'wake up' children who are feeling tired or 'out of sorts'. Our list includes a snack, a drink, short period of exercise in the fresh air, washing face or brain gym. Of course to begin with the children invariably chose the first two. Sometimes these worked but often they did not, that is the children were still not settling and tackling work well, so I was able to comment on this and steer them towards trying the other strategies.

This activity enables us to teach the vocabulary and concepts of emotions and also to raise the children's level of awareness in line with Sensory Integration ideas. We use some brain gym ideas coupled with short, energizing techniques and relaxation techniques first thing in the morning after looking at our feelings board, but also throughout the day. These are also especially useful after play and dinner breaks.

There are one or two children in my class who find it very difficult to sit still for any length of time so I try to stretch and move the whole group every now and then but also have some other agreed procedures.

- **Moving breaks**. A child is allowed to have a quiet walk round, look out of the window for a few moments, walk to toilets and wash hands and come back; that is stretch their legs for a short time. We practised this and talked about it a lot before it became an established and non-disruptive routine and it certainly seems to help.
- **'Brain gym'**. This is intended wake up the brain, and my children like this. There are various exercises that are supposed to stimulate thinking. Here are three:
  Rub ear lobes then roll them up and down.
  Draw large sideways figure eights in the air, right hand, then left hand, then both hands together. (If you teach the children to keep their heads still but track their thumb nail with their eyes only, this doubles as a visual tracking exercise.)
  Energy yawn – massage muscles where lower jaw meets upper jaw in front of ear. This invariably makes you yawn, which you enjoy. Then take an energizing breath – place hands on table, or if standing, loosely by sides. Lower chin to chest, relax/make shoulders floppy, feel the gentle stretch in the back of the neck. Take a deep slow breath in through nose while gently lifting chin up and then putting head back, allowing back to arch slightly and so opening rib cage. Then exhale through mouth while curving the back and bringing chin back to rest on chest. A couple of these are a real wake-up.

4

- **Mini relaxation**. Standing or sitting straight and tall but relaxed/floppy shoulders, arms, hands. (It can help to teach the children to put their hands loosely together or to put finger and thumb loosely together with other fingers curled.) Close eyes and take three slow but very quiet breaths in through nose and out through mouth with a quiet sigh.

Behaviour

Every school needs to have a well-established and clearly understood discipline and bullying policy in place. This should include:

- clear rules and routines within a climate of mutual respect and clear expectations;
- clear system of rewards and sanctions, including a time-out 'thinking' area in class and a time-out system for beyond the classroom;
- attractive and well-organized environment with adequate resources for differentiated curriculum;
- a set of procedures including tactical ignoring, reminders of rules, questioning, giving choices, direction, warnings, redirecting to defuse a situation, using time out, setting up personal behaviour agreements if necessary and using a team approach to solving persistent behaviour problems.

However, some children with SLI and with other impairments will need more than this. They may need to understand what is not acceptable alongside what is acceptable. They may need to practise acceptable behaviours. With unacceptable behaviours we have found it necessary to state their unacceptability, firmly but calmly, then to demonstrate what would be acceptable in that situation. This usually needs thinking through carefully, as most children will follow the examples given literally.

Different situations require different behaviours and some children will need reteaching for each new location or each new set of circumstances. Using the principles of Carol Gray's *Social Stories*, we also write personal books for some children, addressing particular behaviour, and use them to teach and then to be read to, and by, the children. Photocopiable ones have proved most useful as they are used for whole-class teaching and discussion and copies are also sent home for use there. We have found those that state what **not to do** alongside what **to do** are most effective. The example below was part of lots of work on playing kindly and gently so that this vocabulary was clearly understood.

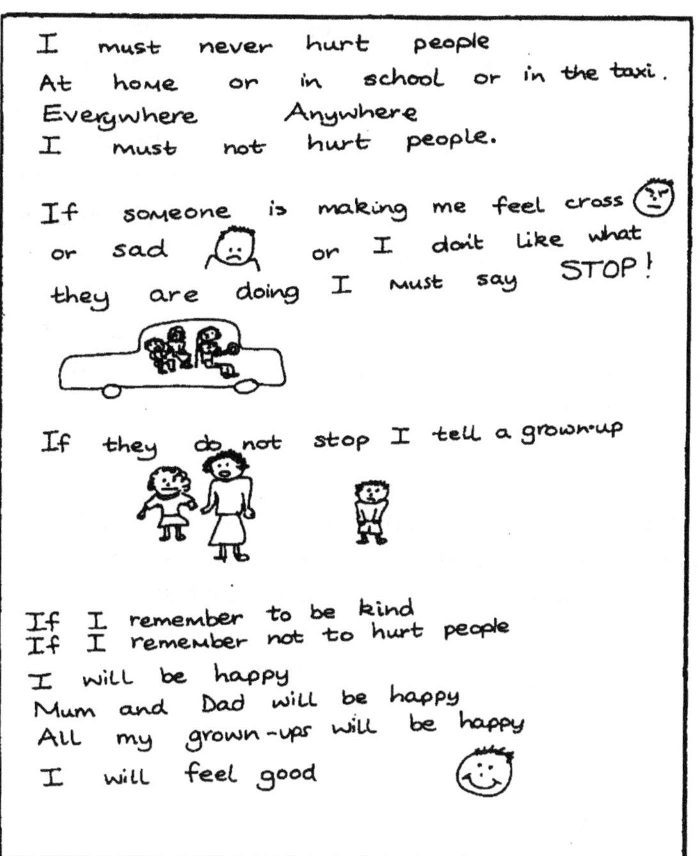

It has proved helpful with older children to further explore a range of strategies for breaks and lunchtimes. Discuss the rules and procedures for these times. Discuss strategies for joining a group, leaving a group and possible responses to peer-group language. Discuss possible strategies for dealing with teasing and bullying: it will help if each child has a plan ready to use. Again it is most helpful if this is approached as a whole-school issue, with procedures in place for all. However, pupils with social language difficulties will need additional, direct teaching on how to respond, behave appropriately and keep safe in a range of situations. At school much of this work can be carried out with peers through circle time activities, drama and role-play.

Discuss with the pupil(s) how in some situations they will not understand what is meant and will not be able to make themselves understood. Discuss possible strategies:

- 'I'm not very good with words'/'I don't understand'/'Could you write it down please?'
- 'Can you tell me another way please?'
- 'I'll just leave it for now thank you.'
- Phone home for help. Teach them always to check that they have money and/or a pre-paid phone card for the phone. As a back-up teach them how to make a reverse charge call.
- Sometimes in peer-group situations it may be best to walk away. If appropriate, AFASIC produces a smart, unobtrusive plastic card that briefly but clearly explains the holder's difficulties with

language. (There are a number of books with ideas for activities in the Books and Resources section, including Wendy Rinaldi's *Social Use of Language Programme.*) Interventions are most effective if parents are involved as well, contributing to a united approach by school and home, and it may also be useful for children to attend out-of-school clubs such as Rainbows, Beavers, gymnastics or swimming.

Personal organization, or lack of it, can have a significant impact on children's ability to cope in the classroom, and therefore on their resulting behaviour. It is important for teachers to explicitly reward good organization:

- at the table, organizing books, pencil, personal dictionary, ruler, etc., including getting them out and putting them away;
- taking care of own belongings - book bag, PE kit, sandwich box, etc.;
- taking responsibility for specific jobs around class:
- Remembering to bring in items needed for art or other curriculum work.

4

There are some simple items that may make life easier for older children and points which parents can be made aware of:

- A smart notebook, a Filofax, a very small cassette recorder or electronic organizer - whatever is 'in vogue' - in which to jot things that may otherwise be forgotten such as messages for parents or homework, party invitations, trips, etc. It can also contain vital information such as personal addresses, phone numbers and emergency plans for who to phone and where to go when things go wrong.
- Instead of parents remembering and packing games kit, swimming kit, etc. children should learn to do so themselves. Have a weekly timetable in a conspicuous place that is checked at a regular time every day. Pack school bags the evening before after checking the timetable.
- Suggest that parents buy a talking watch for children with difficulties understanding time. These are available from The RNIB, PO Box 173, Peterborough, PE2 6WS.
- Lack of awareness of possible difficulties and dangers make road safety training an absolute priority for teachers and parents. RoSPA has some very useful resources (RoSPA House, Edgbaston Park, 353 Bristol Road, Edgbaston, Birmingham B5 7ST or online at www.rospa.org.uk/resources).
- It is useful to have a basic toolkit for school. This might include pens, felts, calculator, inhaler, etc. and it should be the child's responsibility to organize replacements. Sometimes it is helpful to have two, one for home and homework and one for school.

Turn-taking is another area that many children find difficult. Some well-known games, which also encourage concentration and reasoning, are useful. These could be played at home or school.

- If, from Philip & Tacey Ltd, North Way, Andover, Hants SP10 5BA;
- Guess Who, from Hasbro UK Ltd, Caswell Way, Newport, Gwent NP9 0YH; also available from any Early Learning Centre;
- Connect Four;
- Mastermind;
- Taboo;
- Trivial Pursuit.

There are many more that could be used to suit different ages.

Sequencing in time and space can also be problematical. This includes difficulties with before/after, days, months, seasons, positional vocabulary and ordering and retelling events.

- Positional vocabulary activities will need to continue into Key Stage 2 and beyond.
- Calendar work, which goes on daily in most classrooms at Key Stage 1, will need to continue into Key Stage 2 and beyond. Regularly chant the days, the day before/yesterday and the day after/tomorrow. Associate regular activities with each day – Monday is the first day of the week and writing day, Tuesday is PE, etc. Regularly chant or sing the months and seasons and build up to each child saying his birthday – 'My birthday is on the 31st of May, in the Spring.'

  It is most useful to have a calendar at home to help the child check and assemble equipment ready for the next day [See Appendix 6]. If movable arrows are used (Blu-tack or adhesive Velcro are most useful) calendars can also help alleviate feelings of panic and disorientation that some children with SLI feel on waking each day. Using a movable arrow the day can be highlighted and regular events can be noted down for reference.
- Sequencing activities can be included in most curriculum areas as part of differentiated work.
- Concrete references, activities and pictorial charts will be needed for a considerable time by some children.

Sunday	Monday	Tuesday	Wednesday	Thursday	Friday	Saturday
	1	1	1	1	1	
	2	2	2	2	2	
	3	3	3	3	3	
	4	4	4	4	4	
	5	5		5	5	
	At home	**At home**	**At home**	**At home**	**At home**	
Pack swimming kit Check that all homework is done	Do homework for: Pack PE kit	Do homework for: Pack PE kit	Do homework for: Collect materials	Do homework for: Pack Karate kit	Do homework for: Pack PE kit	Make sure all sports kit and school uniform is washed
Dinner money						
Bus fare/pass						

5 Developmental Co-ordination Difficulties

Some children with speech and language impairment also have co-ordination difficulties, sometimes termed dyspraxia or developmental co-ordination difficulties (DCD). As with speech and language impairment, DCD encompass a range of problems:

D irection
E mbarrassment
V isual perception
m **E** mory, listening
L aterality
O ral motor skills
P lanning, proprioception, pain
M ovement
E motion (impulsive or low arousal levels)
N ormal intelligence
T actile system affected
A uditory processing, attention
re **L** ationships

(With kind permission of Amanda Hopkin, Head Paediatric Occupational Therapist, Maelor Children's Centre, Wrexham)

This is a wide-ranging list that incorporates sensory integration difficulties. The overlap with SLI can clearly be seen and so some of the areas affected have already been covered. In addition, the vestibular and the proprioceptive systems may be working inefficiently. The vestibular system is the processing of information on gravity and balance through the inner ear. The proprioceptive system is the processing of information about body parts and body position through muscles, ligaments and nerves.

Some children may have an inefficient sensory intake and therefore actively seek extra sensory stimulation. Such children are moving and fidgeting all the time, they fiddle with things and may often end up breaking them. They act impulsively and tend to get messy with food or paint, and their clothes become twisted and untucked, though they will probably not notice this at all.

Conversely, some children may routinely take in too much sensory information and so avoid sensory stimuli. These children may not walk up and down stairs confidently, they dislike climbing frames and slides, are easily overwhelmed by movement and may well be travel-sick. They may avoid certain smells and tastes in foods and may be picky eaters.

If these difficulties are severe then advice can be sought from the Physiotherapy Service or Occupational Therapy Service. They may be able to offer some physiotherapy sessions and, if appropriate, a programme. However, many therapy services are overstretched and less severe problems can be targeted regularly in school both in discrete sessions and as a warm-up in PE. Short, regular sessions have proved successful for some children. We take a whole-school approach to this at Acton Park Infants School, and pupils from mainstream classes join in with some from the language class to follow a daily exercise programme. This programme is described on pages 43–47. Parents can supervise or join in with some exercises and can encourage ball play, skipping, bike riding, etc. Some children benefit greatly from attending swimming, golf, gym or dance clubs.

Fine motor

Some children also have fine motor difficulties and generally need extra practice at threading, cutting, tracing, painting, etc. These can usually be fitted in to the school day at primary level; short, regular sessions have proved most successful. Activities can be practised at home too.

5

- Encourage short, daily finger-flexing exercises – there are a number of these in our motor programme given below. It is most useful to do some of these before a writing session.
- Offer a range of pens and pencils.
- Pencil grips and, for older children, triangular shaped pencils can help. ('Tri-go' is LDA's pencil grip and it is an excellent design.)
- Cardboard, finger-shaped finger spaces with a dab of Blu-tack on the back can be used to help establish good spacing. They eventually become redundant.
- Offer a range of scissors – left and right-handed, spring-loaded and very sharp for cutting fabric.
- A sloped desktop that fits on school tables is useful. Construct one from a file or purchase one from a number of suppliers. For older children there are some that fit discreetly into an A4 folder.
- Provide active demonstration of, and then regular practice at, good sitting at a table. We have a short chant – bottom back, feet flat (and hands in your lap). Posture cushions are very helpful for some children and there is a range available. (Movin'sit, from Gymnic, is triangular and fits neatly on to school chairs. It has a raised, knobbly surface that really helps those children with proprioceptive difficulties as they can move about more discreetly.) Some children will then need footrests so that their feet can be flat. These can be simply made from telephone

directories or catalogues. Establish the correct positioning for right- and left-handers.

- Set up and encourage or direct the use of a hand gym with things such as bubble wrap to pop, pegs and bulldog clips to open and shut, multi-link and pop-it beads to fix together.
- Use a handwriting system and recognize that some children will need daily practice, then regular practice for a lot longer than other children. Older children may find paper with raised marker lines helpful (available from Philip & Tacey). Some children may also respond better to cursive script and to pen, rather than pencil, or to using a keyboard. Keyboards are cumbersome for note-taking in class however, and it is more successful to have lesson notes provided for some children who then use the keyboard to redraft these and make them their own.
- Teach simple folk dances, which are good fun, develop listening skills and a sense of rhythm and are a way of learning and practising using right and left hands. I give our young children a ponytail band to put on their right wrist to help them remember which is their right hand. (A range of folk dance music that comes with instructions is available from Folk in Education, details in the Books and Resources section.)

Motor-skills development programme

Plan to have a short session of about ten minutes each day if possible, or at least twice a week. The following set of exercises is a guide. Please contact the author at jillmcminn.public@bigfoot.com for further examples. Obviously, staff need to assess their pupil's current performance and difficulties and then draw up an appropriate programme. This set of exercises starts at crawling and not all groups will need to start at this basic level. Be flexible and respond to the progress the children are making, particular difficulties and also to moods (theirs and yours). I tend to use the same set of exercises for at least a week, but sometimes longer. My mainstream colleague likes to work at one or two tasks exclusively until progress is evident. There are many ways of organizing the sessions. We use the school hall at changeover times for the ten minutes when it is not in use while PE or other classes are changing or getting organized, so there is no infringement of precious hall time. If the weather is good we go outside in the fresh air and also to use the concrete steps to walk up and down.

Establish a routine for starting and finishing the session; I tend to keep the same one for several weeks. Our current beginning routine is standing relaxation. Good standing (straight and tall, feet slightly apart, eyes open, arms loosely down by sides and feel as if there's a string tied to the top of the head gently pulling you tall and straight) with eyes closed and breathing quietly in through nose and out through mouth, three breaths. Our current ending routine is good standing, then walking out of the hall either on toes or on heels – children choose which way.

An alternative is: good standing, then flop forwards from the waist like a floppy doll, dangle for a few seconds then uncurl back to upright. Good standing, shake hands vigorously. Slowly and carefully drop head to one shoulder, hold, roll head back to midpoint, hold, drop head to other shoulder, hold and back to midpoint. Gently roll head round. Good standing, hands holding sides at bottom of ribcage, breathe in through nose and out through mouth, finishing with a deep breath in and out. Good standing, shake hands vigorously.

Relaxation techniques, both sitting and lying down, can also be used as a finishing routine. Good sitting, legs crossed, back straight but not tense, then chin tipped down to throat, eyes closed and backs of wrists on knees, fingers loosely curled, quiet breathing. Lying on back, legs slightly apart, hands down by sides, palms up, fingers loosely curled, eyes closed.

It is important when finishing with relaxation to 'wake the body up' before moving back to class: shake arms, legs, one at a time, then whole body, then stretch up.

5

We assess in an ongoing manner by observing children each day in the sessions and in and around school. We update the record sheets more precisely about once a term by going through the activities and noting down how each child is doing. A sample record sheet is given on p. 48.

In our specialist language class we also use PE warm-up times to practise the above skills. We carry out the hand and finger exercises regularly in class before writing and have a shoe box 'hand gym' that the children use in class. We also incorporate rhythm, clapping and tapping exercises in our music and listening activities and a range of manipulative skills within classwork. All these complement the work carried out in the daily exercise sessions.

Repeat the exercise three, five, or ten times as appropriate and as time allows.

1. Starting routine.
2. In prone position, lying flat on stomach, arms bent with elbow to palm flat on floor, hands level with shoulders. Lie straight. Lift head slowly, hold, then slowly lower.
3. As 2. Lift head and top of trunk.
4. On hands and knees hold balance then rock back onto heels and forward again.
5. Good crawling.
6. Creeping on hands and feet.

7. Stand straight and tall, put arms out sideways at shoulder level, spin round, then stand and gain balance. If steady, can try with eyes closed.
8. Stand straight and tall, with left hand touch right shoulder, elbow, knee, foot and then with right hand touch left shoulder, elbow, knee, foot.
9. Finishing routine.

We also have sessions using balls and beanbags for throwing, catching, rolling, spinning, dribbling, etc, and, if appropriate, we work directly on learning our right and left hand, though this is often left to Key Stage 2.

Assessment

(This will probably take more than one session.)

1. Starting routine.
2. As teacher calls out to move in various ways – good walking, walk on toes, heels, heel to toe, jump, hop, etc., stopping when teacher calls stop.
3. Balancing on various body parts for countdown from ten (one leg, each leg in turn, bottom, hand and leg, knees . . .).
4. Rocking. Standing, sway from side to side and forwards and backwards. Lying on back rock from side to side. On knees sway from side to side and forwards and backwards.
5. Children choose to sit or lie down and with eyes closed touch body parts as teacher calls them out quite quickly.
6. With ball throw and catch, bounce and catch, dribble and stop with foot.
7. With bean bag move from hand to hand in front, over and under each leg in turn, over shoulder to other hand then up and round front back to first hand, eyes open, then eyes closed.
8. Cross lateral. Crawling, creeping on hands and feet, opposite arm and leg stretched out in front, right hand to left shoulder, elbow, knee, toe and vice versa and 'cat's got the measles' (good standing, then jump and cross legs at ankles, then jump apart).
9. Finishing routine.

(See record chart on page 48.)

Hand and finger exercises

If appropriate, I try to establish the habit of using dominant hand first in these exercises, so right-handers will use right hand first and left-handers use left hand first. This is difficult with young children who have no secure understanding of right and left so I use 'pencil hand' and 'not pencil hand' or having each child put a hair band round the right wrist, 'band hand' and 'other hand' to begin with.

1. Hold a pencil ready to write; keeping hand, arm and shoulder still, move the finger and thumb that are holding the pencil backwards and forwards in a 'frog's legs' movement. This movement is key to easy handwriting without aches and pains in arms and shoulders.
2. Establish good sitting, with chair close enough to table, sitting back in chair with feet flat on floor. Shrug, then rotate shoulders to relax posture. Shake arms down by sides.
3. Palms together, fingers spread, press fingers together and push elbows out with heel of hands down.
4. Fingers interlaced, stretch both arms in front and push palms forwards.
5. Monkey grip – interlock fingers of one hand with the fingers of the other hand. Pull apart for five seconds, then release for five seconds. Repeat three to five times.
6. Open and close fingers, stretching them on the open movement.
7. Make a fist of each hand, then vigorously flick fingers out.
8. Slowly curl fingers closed, then slowly curl them open.
9. Fingers curled, point with each finger in turn, right hand then left hand.
10. Typing/piano playing – both hands with forearms resting on table. The typewriter keys/piano keys need to be hit quite hard with separate fingers.
11. Paper scrunch – start with tissue and then try newspaper or other paper that requires more strength. Start at one corner with the writing hand; gather all the paper into a tight ball. Throw it into the bin for target practice.
12. Move the pencil – hold pencil in the air, with the writing hand, grasping it at one end. Try to wriggle the hand up to the other end of the pencil using finger movement. Then try to move it back to the original position.
13. Pencil windmill – hold pencil in the air, with the writing hand, and try to turn it like a windmill, using only the hand that is holding the pencil. Try clockwise and anti-clockwise.
14. Hold a pen top, or similar short cylindrical object, between thumb and index and middle fingers and try to turn it round and round clockwise, then anti-clockwise. Then try rolling it down to the base of the thumb/fingers and back up to the top.
15. Right hand then left hand (vice versa if left-handed), press each finger in turn to tip of thumb. Then try both hands together. Eyes open, then eyes closed.
16. Put sticky tape on the pad of the index finger, with a bit of tape protruding. Try to get the tape off, using each of the other fingers of the same hand in turn. Repeat with other hand.
17. Place a rubber band over the fingers and the thumb in a loose but just firm fit. Wriggle the fingers and thumb 'open and shut'/together and apart to get the band off.To begin with put the rubber band near the top of the digits then lower down as skill increases. Try different combinations – one finger and thumb, two fingers and thumb, two adjoining fingers ...

18. Pressing elbows to sides, point hands and fingers forwards, then one hand at a time rotate hand from wrist, keeping rest of body still.
19. Arm distance from wall, place hands palm down flat to wall and press down on palms and fingers, then use fingers to push back upright. This can be repeated using a table.
20. Place palm flat on table, raise one finger at a time. One hand at a time, then both together.
21. Put hands flat on table, keep fingers straight and move the index finger away from the middle finger, then the index and middle fingers away from the ring finger, then the little finger away from the other fingers. Repeat several times.
22. Hold thumb and next two fingers in cutting/position, as if using scissors, and practise scissor/cutting movement.
23. Rub hands/fingers briskly.
24. Elbows on table, press heels of hands together, curl fingers, tips apart, then touch corresponding tips one at a time. Eyes open then eyes closed.
25. Sometimes it is helpful to do good sitting, then let chin drop to chest, shoulders droop, close eyes and breathe quietly before starting to write.

Record chart

Key

J: Jerky, heavy footed, not flowing or controlled
S: Sustains pose or movements for ? seconds
D: Needing demonstration and reminder
W: Wobbly, arms or hands waving or up in hypertensive position, losing balance easily
F: Arms flailing

Name

	Date	Date	Date
Good crawling, creeping			
Good standing			
Walks steadily			
Can walk on toes			
Can walk on heels			
Along line/bench			
Up/down steps alternate feet			
Heel to toe			
Standing leg balance			
Standing leg swing			
Stand circle toes in air			
Good balance on knees			
Bridge			
Good sitting			
Good stand from sitting & v v			
Squat balance/bounce			
Rock in swan position bwrds/fwrds			
Curled on back rock side to side			
Sit & spin			
Standing twist			
Cat's got measles			
Shoulder raise singly & both tog			
Shoulder fwrds & bwrds singly & both tog			
Standing scissor arm swing			
Arm rotation			
Straight arm stretch			
Sustained hops			
Sustained jumps			
Skips			
Skips with rope			
Throw, catch, bounce ball			
Finger flex			
Finger curl			
Close fingers smoothly on to palm starting with little finger			
Fingers to thumb, one at time			
Elbows to waist, arms parallel to ground rotate wrists			
Kneeling hands flat on floor rock fwrd weight on wrists			
Cross lateral exercises			
Relax, be still			

6 Curriculum

It will be clear that the speech and language difficulties described so far will directly affect learning in all areas of the curriculum.

Speech production

It may be hard to understand what a child is saying when he/she is:

- joining in class or group discussions;
- answering questions;
- asking questions;
- reading his/her own work or other texts;
- spelling out loud.

It may therefore be more difficult for a child to show what he or she knows and for the teacher to assess progress.

Vocabulary

Some children will have great difficulty with specific curriculum vocabulary:

- pronouncing – 'manget' for magnet, 'ecectrility' for electricity;
- understanding – left can mean gone or remaining, or the opposite to right;
- remembering;
- spelling;
- recognizing and using particular words or operational signs, patterns, shapes, place value, the decimal point and numerators/ denominators.

Grammar

Words and word parts may be omitted, letters, words and sentences jumbled when a child is:

- joining in class or group discussions;
- answering questions;
- asking questions;
- reading aloud;
- spelling out loud;
- recording curriculum work.

Listening and understanding

Some children will have great difficulty in:

- focusing at the start of a lesson;
- processing, understanding, remembering all the given information;
- following instructions during the lesson.

Memory

Some children will have great difficulty in trying to remember facts. This can cause panic and overload and result in a total loss of focus on the lesson or task. They may have problems with:

- sequences of instructions;
- specific vocabulary and facts;
- recalling different information, which makes it difficult for them to link subjects across the curriculum area and hinders their problem-solving ability.

Social use of language

Behaviour in class, including class, group and paired discussion and working may be affected as some children will have difficulty in:

- understanding and remembering different routines or codes within each class, possibly resulting in a difficulty with settling down;
- relating to others and behaving appropriately with others;
- remembering and using turn-taking procedures and ways of contributing in class.

Developmental co-ordination

Some children will have great difficulty in:

- drawing pictures or diagrams, copying from a board, book or workcard;
- writing words or numbers correctly;
- handling and using equipment including scissors, pencils, pens, rubbers and rulers and other measuring tools;
- differentiating between right and left, and so have problems writing on lines left to right and top to bottom on a page;
- deciding what equipment they need and organizing all equipment in their working space so they have enough room to work.
- appreciating sequential pattern, and sequencing the findings of an investigation;
- identifying similar words – see/seeds, wet/went ...

These are generic problems that all teaching staff need to understand. The following sections cover some subject-specific ideas.

English

Speaking and listening

All the games and activities described in Chapters 2 and 3 can be part of speaking and listening work.

Reading

- It is possible for unintelligible children to be reading accurately but to be unable to articulate the words. This is a tricky area but there is no need to hold up reading experience if your instinct indicates that they are reading accurately. Understanding and recall of sight vocabulary can be checked and developed using visual skills - matching, highlighting, pointing to, etc.
- Collect and create simple teacher-made books with target vocabulary or grammar in them. We have a set of concept books on wet/dry, hard/soft, colours, and some teacher-made books that start at a very early sentence level - Mum is walking, the boy is writing, etc. Some children will make a start with simple, personally designed books. Have available as wide a range of books as possible, sorted along Reading Recovery lines into stages that increase in difficulty in very small steps with lots of repetition.
- The Paget Gorman signing system, which was designed to support the development of spoken language in children with speech and language impairment, actively helps with the learning of a core sight vocabulary. It gives a visual clue and support can be given without interrupting the flow of reading, particularly with words such as '**in, the, is**' and confusions such as '**was/went**'.
- Traditional tales and nursery rhymes frequently feature in school readers so it is useful to give these extra attention. Some children may not have heard them much and others may have heard them but do not readily recall them. We regularly take these as our topic theme, and plan a range of curriculum work around it.
- Story tapes - these are available for all ages with or without accompanying books. It can also be of great benefit to some children to use teacher-made tapes that are linked to current classwork.
- It is very important to check understanding - some children can decode well so seem to be reading well but are not reading with understanding. They need lots of practice at answering simple questions (Appendix 4), predicting what will happen next and retelling the story.
- Some text layouts are more difficult to follow than others, so keep this in mind when selecting suitable reading books.
- Some children will have great difficulty recalling character names, place names and previous events as well as core words.

Be ready to support the flow of reading by reminding the child of these words, before he starts to read. During reading, if a given clue does not trigger recall, then tell the child the word to keep the flow of the reading and make the reading session more enjoyable. Then plan for some practice of target names at another time. Acknowledge the child's memory difficulties in a positive way, as outlined earlier. Set realistic targets about teaching techniques for decoding and developing a core sight vocabulary.

- Some children may have difficulties tracking across a page or focusing on words, and for some the words may move around or flicker. If a child appears to be having difficulty or screws up his eyes a lot, or his eyes water a lot when reading, then suggest to parents that they arrange for a sight test. Simple eye exercises can help, and some children have tinted glasses. Try using a tracker - these can be bought from a supplier, or make them out of a rectangle of card with an opening cut in the centre. You can use this to outline a sentence, or two or three sentences, by adjusting the size of the opening. You can also try different colours of cellophane paper to make your own filters.
- Help the children to organize their reading equipment by having a regular routine. Teach them what should be in their book bag or rucksack, and when it should be in school. Reward them when they remember.

Writing

Use shared contexts or given inputs to start with, to help in understanding exactly what those children with speech production difficulties are saying when they are reading back their work.

6

- Teach a core written vocabulary.
- Be realistic about how many spellings and how much grammar you expect to be correct, depending on each child's difficulties and targets. Obviously you will have a teaching programme for spelling and grammar in place.
- Use a structured dictionary system.
  This may start with a 'Breakthrough to Literacy' approach, so the children can make sentences with support and read them to a few friends before copying them. Cardboard finger spaces can be used alongside the cardboard words to encourage spaces to be left when copying writing. Move on to using a teacher-made open personal dictionary (Appendix 5). These dictionaries can be used in a number of ways. Children can finger-trace words using a look, cover, write method while they are learning a core written vocabulary. They can find their own words and later the initial letter of words. They can begin to try their own spelling.
- Picture sequences can be used at first to retell stories. Tell the story and let the children act it out the day before, or some days before the writing, to develop memory skills. In this way

children become confident as they have something to write about and they can build up a repertoire of storylines. When they are confident at this you can try:

changing a character, a setting, an event . . .;

demonstrating how to storyboard the story with the changes (using blank cartoon-type boxes to draw the key events of the story).

- When the children are confident at retelling and changing in this way, move on to story planning with storyboards, using a single picture/event/item as a stimulus. Some children need to be specifically taught how to do quick pictures or else they will spend all the available time drawing. Most children with SLI need support while practising how to write their story from a storyboard.
- Narrative packs and oral storytelling
  The narrative packs produced by Black Sheep Press offer a detailed oral approach into the concepts and structure needed for storytelling. The activities work through the individual components of a simple story, to retelling and then to generating ideas for stories using the questions 'Who?', 'What?', 'Where?' and 'When?' This can be linked with encouraging pupils to tell a story that is then acted out at story time; based on Vivian Gussin-Paley's work. These two approaches together can in turn be linked to story writing, giving it a meaningful and clearly understood foundation.
- When the children start to try their own spellings give them a 'Have-a-Go' book. This encourages independent spelling, keeps a record of spelling progression and enables discussion and use of correct spelling.
- As often as possible, encourage the children to talk through what they are going to write a number of times: before they start, during the writing, and at the finish to check they have kept to their plan. They can also be encouraged to check they have included all words and maybe choose one or two spellings that they have had a good try with but recognize do not look correct.
- Show the children what to do with lots of teacher-led writing demonstrations, using examples that they can then refer to during the writing process.
- Use writing frames for different kinds of writing – letters, poems, informational writing – and/or dictionary sheets to support these.
- Read lots of different poetry to the children and show them it doesn't always rhyme. Using cloze is useful, with the children filling in specific words in a given framework. Alternatively, use large strips of paper and during the input write down exactly what each child says, using the kind of prompting outlined earlier in the Expressive Language – Vocabulary section.
- Introduce the children to written recipes during cookery sessions and use a recipe format to write a poem e.g. Autumn – Take a

cupful of conkers, a tablespoon of yellow leaves, a tablespoon of red leaves . . .

- Use ICT: we have recently purchased Clicker 4, which enables personal screens to be set up for each pupil. It is like an on-screen concept keyboard and it is a big advantage since it has speech and graphics and can be used for a range of curriculum work.
- Older pupils may benefit from portable, tabletop vocabulary reference charts and story-planning charts.
- Give experience of different styles of writing and purposes for writing - thank-you letter, postcard, etc. and link to social skills being covered. Linking this to role-play with younger children is very useful.

Spelling

In my class rhythm and rhyme work are seen as the first stage of spelling.

Rhythm work. Some activities were given earlier in the 'Expressive Language - Speech Production' section. Here are some more:

- tapping out children's names;
- tapping out a selection of words with different numbers of syllables;
- tapping out words from current topic vocabulary;
- tapping different rhythm patterns in music;
- moving the whole body to different rhythms in folk and modern dance.

As the children become adept at tapping syllables a recording system can be used whereby a counter or pencil mark is put on a grid for each syllable. Later this system can be used to show the number of letters in a word.

Rhyme work. Our experience and current research has shown the importance of rhyme.

- Listen to and learn nursery rhymes and other age-appropriate rhymes.
- Play about with well-known rhymes and make up new possibilities, e.g. Humpty-Dumpty sat on a chair/rug/dish, etc. Humpty-Dumpty had curly hair/a new mug/a big fish, etc.
- Recite nursery rhymes leaving a space for the group to recite the missing rhyming word - Jack and Jill went up the —.
- Recite nursery rhymes but put in the wrong word and children have to stand up if they hear a wrong word, then tell you what it was - Jack and Jill went up the stairs, etc.
- Reverse words - Song a sing of sixpence/Jill and Jack went up the hill.

- Substitute words – Baa baa purple sheep/Twinkle, twinkle little car.
- Swap word order – Humpty-Dumpty wall on a sat/Jack fell down and crown his broke.
- Swap word parts – 1,2 shuckle my boo/I'm a little teapot, shawl and tout/Incy wincy spider went up the spater wout.
- Rhyming pairs or snap. Identify and chant the rhymes together first, then take turns round the circle to pick up two cards at a time looking for the pairs. Or give one card to each child (making sure there are pairs of rhyming words); the first child stands and says his/her word, e.g. 'hat', and the child with the rhyming card stands and says his/her rhyme, then all chant the rhyme.
- Use rhyming picture cards. Lay them out face up. Start the game by saying 'I need a word that rhymes with hat.' The children look for rhyming cards (have more than one if possible) and put hands up to identify. You could have counters and award a counter for each one found.
- 'My basket is full of **cheese**.' One child says the line then throws a beanbag to a friend who says it again but gives a different rhyme (peas, fleas, trees, bees, keys, or any nonsense rhyme – mees, rees . . .) Other starter lines:
  My basket is full of logs
  My basket is full of hats
  My basket is full of cars, etc.
- Rhyming I spy. I spy something that rhymes with ball.
- Give a rhyme – Ask the children as a group or in turn to fill in the rhyme.

On a log I saw a..............................	The boy is tall he can catch the.............
I like to eat a slice of	Tears in my eye I started to..................
The pig wore a...............................	My sock is on the.............................
The star is in the	I saw a rat chasing a ....
When we go for a walk I like to...........	The rich king wore a sparkling...............
A fox in a......................................	A green snake eating ....
Do you see the little..........................	On a dark night the moon shines ....
I saw a mole come out of a................	6,7,8 shut the...................................
The little hen swallowed a..................	Stop singing that song it's much too ....
In a house a little............................	In the sun he had some.......................

6

Slightly harder, extended listening and processing.

It is dark, switch on the light. The sun has set now it's....................	This is a word that rhymes with jar. It needs petrol, it is a..........................
You live in me. I sound like mouse. I have a roof and walls. I am a............	This is a word that rhymes with king. It ties things up, it's a ball of.................
You look at me to tell the time. I rhyme with rock I am a....................	This is a word that rhymes with sighs. You see with these, they are your............
I swim in the river, I sound like dish. I am a..	This is a word that rhymes with run. Round and sticky it is a........................
You sit on me I sound like hair. I am a..	This is a word that rhymes with coat. It sails on the sea it is a......................
This is a word that rhymes with make. It's delicious to eat it is a...................	This is a word that rhymes with smelly. It wobbles and wobbles it's delicious.........

After that, or alongside that, a system that teaches letter names, a range of common letter sounds and both upper and lower case has been successful. This emphasizes that most letters have more than one common sound. This has been found particularly important with children who have difficulty understanding language and who interpret literally. If they learn that /a/ says 'a' as in apple they will have difficulty accepting it makes other sounds. It is easier to use '**a**pple begins with **a**', '**a**pron begins with **a** (**ay**)' and to mention that the letter 'a' makes many other sounds as well. To this end we start with a wider group of letter/sound combinations and go on to an even wider set later. Jolly Phonics, a system with visual cues, has also proved most helpful but we have adapted it to include extra actions to go with the additional letter sounds as described above.

6

There are many spelling systems about; *Alpha to Omega* by Bevé Hornsby *et al.* has proved a useful reference. Older pupils have successfully used a package called *Toe by Toe* by Keda Cowling.

- Use multi-sensory techniques whereby letters are looked at, finger traced, traced on a range of rough and smooth surfaces, traced with eyes open and closed.
- Link speech articulation work with spelling.
  Use phonological awareness tasks.
- Count the syllables in a word.
- Count the letters/sounds in a word.
- Subtract a syllable, e.g. farmyard without farm or into without in. Change the first letter but keep the rhyme/word family – cat to hat/rat/sat . . .
- Link handwriting and spelling. A cursive style from the start has been shown to be really helpful. However, I have found that it is necessary at Key Stage 1 to point out the difference between the

way we write the letters and the ways we read them. We have adapted our alphabet reference cards and our core word reference cards to show cursive and non-cursive and we say 'This is the way we read it; this is the way we write it.'

- Use grids, at first with the correct number of boxes, for spelling particular words.
- Use a range of different letters – plastic, magnetic, foam, cardboard.
- Use teacher-made spellers with cardboard letters attached to a base alphabet by sticky-backed Velcro. We sing the alphabet names, sing a vowel song, practise the common initial sounds of the letters as above and pull off the letters to spell words, chanting the names then the sounds, then the whole word.

cat – see (C) ay (A) tee (T) – /c/ /a/ /t/ cat

The nature of speech and language impairment changes over time and some children with early speech production problems, along with children with other language impairment, go on to have more significant literacy difficulties, sometimes called SpLD (specific learning difficulties) or dyslexia. Whatever it is called, these children will need specific help with literacy for a considerable time, maybe for all their schooling.

Mathematics

The language of mathematics

For many children the actual numerical or spatial work involved in the curriculum is obscured by the language surrounding it. It is therefore essential to spend time on the explicit teaching of mathematical vocabulary and explaining the multiple meanings of the most common words. Plan time for overlearning of vocabulary in literacy as well as therapy and numeracy.

- Note any language used in mathematics that has more than one meaning. For example:
  Volume can mean **level of noise** or **amount of space taken up**.
  Left can mean **gone** or **remaining**.
  Place can mean **where you are** or **place value – change in magnitude**.
  Change can mean **change your clothes** or **change in money** as well as **change this number**, etc.
- If a child is having difficulty consider the language being used, try phrasing it another way and then note the particular mathematics terms causing difficulty so these can be worked on later. Allow these pupils more time, or let them use concrete materials and visual aids for longer. Also consider whether the mathematics task has meaning for the child or whether it is too

6

abstract; try to give real examples or at least use concrete materials.

- Use correct and consistent mathematics terminology, discussing this with pupils. Consider using one term only until a pupil is secure in that process, e.g. use add exclusively at first without using more/plus, etc.
- Try to include short regular practice of mathematics vocabulary and procedures. For example, use register time for each child and each member of staff to place their own bottle top under a packed lunch or dinner sign. The bottle tops represent the people present; the idea of representation is an abstract one and it is helpful to practise it like this. We count how many, how many more and less/fewer; we look for the double number. We chant the double numbers from double one up to double ten and, as the year progresses, we chant a range of terms associated with addition and subtraction.

Packed lunch	Dinner
1	1
1	1
1	
1	

This would be 4 packed lunches, 2 dinners, 6 meals altogether.

The double number is 2 with 2 more packed lunches and 2 less (fewer) dinners.

Using fingers we would all show double 2 is 4, 2+2=4, 2 plus 2 is 4, 2 more than 2 is 4, the total of 2 and 2 is 4, 2 count on 2 is 4, 2 and 2 how many altogether?
And:
Half of 4 is 2, 4-2=2, 2 less than 4 is 2, 4 count back 2 is 2, the difference between 2 and 4 is 2, subtract 2 from 4 the answer is 2.

In this way the children become familiar with the range of terms and, although they are simply chanting at first, they are taking the first steps towards understanding them.

- It may be helpful to break down AT 1 to include vocabulary and concepts necessary for investigative maths [see chart opposite].

	Level 1	Level 2
Making decisions to solve problems	Uses maths for practical tasks. Has used a range of maths materials that has been given.	Selects/uses materials for maths tasks. Selects maths materials for own use.
	Shows interest/involvement in 'finding out'. Talks about practical tasks.	Has experienced different ways of tackling a task. Offers ideas for tackling a task.
Developing mathematical language	Is working hard to learn/ understand a range of maths language. Needs consistent terminology.	Can show understanding of a range of maths language Uses and relates numerals/ maths symbols/maths language in a range of situations.
	Answers closed questions ... Is it full or empty? Is it a circle or a square?	Answers closed questions with a choice of objects ... Which is longer? Which is heaviest?
	Completes statements ... It isn't full, it's________ It isn't heavy, it's________	Answers more open questions. How much/many? What shape/size?
	Makes statements ... It's full. This is a circle.	Responds using maths language to 'Tell me about this'. Asks maths questions.
	Follows simple maths instructions.	Chooses how to record from a given range.
Reasoning	Can continue simple sequences. Can make patterns and simply describe them.	Can continue patterns. Can make patterns and describe them. Can use simple patterns in finding solutions.
	Makes simple predictions by answering appropriately, based on own experience of patterns/ relationships. Do you think this will fit there? Will this balance?	Can appropriately answer 'What would happen if?/Why? questions. If I put this on the scales it will ____________ If I pour this in here it will ____________

- In literacy time practise reading for meaning with mathematics problems and encourage the pupils to expect the text to make sense. Teach the vocabulary involved. Discuss which are the key words/parts of the problem and what the pupil has to do, highlighting the important parts. Use concrete apparatus if needed. When finished, help the pupil to talk through what they did.
- Some children may be easily overwhelmed by the enormity of mental mathematics and problem-solving tasks and will need help to get started. They may have difficulty with 'Why?' and 'How?' questions and need lots of demonstration and practice in

working out what to do to tackle a problem, what operation to use, thinking logically and drawing helpful diagrams. Help pupils clarify their thinking, and select the correct format for recording ideas and solutions.

- Separate number work from more investigative and practical mathematics, as the language content of these will require particular attention. This affects the way commercially produced materials are used.
- Consider layout carefully; sometimes this can be most confusing: 15 –8, 20 –4, 8 –7 all proceed left to right but 'take 8 away from 10' does not.
- Similarly consider the layout of number squares. It is easier to comprehend if the numbers go up a 100 square with 1–10 being on the bottom line so the numbers go up as they increase in size. Using different colours for each line also helps.
- The Slavonic abacus has proved a valuable tool as it uses visual strengths. This abacus enables pupils to 'see' numbers and number bonds to 10, and then to 100. Each row of this 100-bead abacus is divided into two sets of five beads in two colours. This design is based on research that shows most pupils can see four beads at a glance. It is therefore a short jump to seeing five. Then the way is open for the pupil to just see (not to count: to see) six, seven, eight or nine beads. Furthermore, a single row of the Slavonic abacus shows the complement to ten.
- Pay particular attention to mathematics terms that may be easily confused, e.g. 13/30, 14/40, and so on.
- Be ready to provide concrete aids for a considerable time and aim for a multi-sensory teaching/learning style. Use sandpaper or textured number reference charts. Have visual aids (tables, charts, diagrams, calculators) available to prompt the memory or to be used if a pupil just can't remember. Make sure that all equipment matches the age and interest level of the pupils and give it all an acceptable status within class. Try to have several or at least more than one aid and have them available for all to use.
- Use class charts to show a range of mathematicss terms such as add, subtract, multiply, divide and equals or use symbols. Each time a new term is encountered it can be added to the chart.
- Check understanding of left and right and of moving from left to right across the page. Mark right and left on the page; have a right and left reference chart available or put a temporary mark on a pupil's hand. Or show pupils that their left hand makes a capital L when you put it on the table or put a wristband on their right hand.
- Consider the use of some number shortcuts, and actively encourage pupils to give approximate answers against which their eventual answer can be checked.
- Demonstrate and talk through how you reached an answer and ask pupils to talk you through how they have reached an answer. This can show difficulties and some interesting methods you may not be aware of. Obviously, some children will find this

really difficult and that in itself reminds you of the difficulties they have in sequential and logical thinking.

- Some mistakes will be due to memory problems or wordfinding difficulties. Accept this and respond sympathetically.
- Check written work frequently so that mistakes can be dealt with early on and, if possible, before the incorrect methods/answers become ingrained and therefore remembered as correct. And check work early on in a lesson to ensure correct layout and so that there isn't too much rewriting or redrawing if it is incorrect.
- Some pupils will benefit from compiling and using a personal reminder book, which has examples of ways of working a problem and particular mathematics vocabulary with a personal explanation/pictogram.
- Check homework tasks are set out correctly and clearly. Provide ready-prepared sheets where possible rather than expect children to copy from the board.
- Mark the starting point on each page - green for go - and the stopping point - red for stop. Use arrows, dotted lines or colours to show the way to go across or down the page.
- Teach the writing of numerals in groups where numerals that are being confused are not taught at the same time. If particular numerals are being confused, give each one a different identifying attribute - colour or cartoon/picture.
- Allow the use of number stamps, plastic and stick-on numbers while pupils are becoming competent in writing numbers.
- Use different colours for numbers/signs that are confused or place on different coloured card as reference sheets. Or use full arrow shapes for the more and less signs.
- Teach how to use squared paper but continue to use start/stop marker and guides lines, HTU, etc.
- Plan for more pattern work, patterns of numbers that make 10, that make 20, within a 100 square, within tables, etc.
- Practise the days of the week, months, etc. as regularly as possible.
- Teach and practise rounding up/down to the nearest ten, so that estimating is easier.
- Encourage children to work in pencil, as it's easier to rub out and redo. Establish the use of rulers for any lines and give time to practise the correct use of a ruler and other drawing and measuring tools. Purchase rulers with handles to help those with co-ordination difficulties.

Many pupils feel anxious about mathematics and their fears can lead to avoidance strategies, such as doing work very slowly, or disruptive behaviour or even truancy.

- Acknowledge to the pupil that you understand that he or she has to work hard at mathematics and praise the effort he/she is making. Plan for success. Balance set tasks to include a mix of those that pupils can succeed with, and those where support is needed. Have help (visual aids, charts as well as teacher help) organized and available when it is needed.

- Be aware of each pupil's coping strategies and explain these to helpers and parents.
- Avoid asking anxious pupils to answer aloud at first and establish a supportive environment wherein any contribution is welcomed and praised and 'good thinking' is highlighted and discussed.
- Create opportunities for collaborative working.

Each pupil with SLI will present with a different pattern of difficulties and abilities and it is likely that each will have a mix of problems. It will be necessary to establish priorities for each pupil to ensure overlearning and revisiting of vital pre-number and early mathematics knowledge. Some children with speech and language impairment have an aptitude for mathematics computation and experience their first feelings of success with number work, but need particular help with the language of mathematics. Others find all mathematics work extremely difficult and need lots of praise for their courage and the enormous effort they make in tackling it rather than for the end result.

Science

Problem-solving, knowledge of facts and understanding specific terminology are areas that are central to science as well as mathematics. Some children will have difficulty pronouncing science terminology. This in turn will affect their recall, understanding and use of some words. Try to include short regular practice of some vocabulary and use class charts/wall displays to show a range of terms.

Much of the vocabulary and language concepts that underpin science are covered in the First Words list in Appendix 2. It is useful to target specific vocabulary in language sessions as well as science sessions and also to involve parents where possible, in using opportunities to practise the words at home, e.g. same/different, changed/change/change back, longer/shorter, wider/narrower, rougher/smoother.

- As in mathematics some language used in science has more than one meaning. For example:

  Soil can mean **dirty** or **earth**.
  Change can mean change **your clothes** or **change in money** as well as **change this number**, etc.
  Light can mean **not heavy** or **illumination**.

- If a child is having difficulty in understanding the language being used, try phrasing it another way and then note the particular science terms causing difficulty so these can be worked on later. Also consider whether the science task has meaning for the child or whether it is too abstract; try to give real examples or use concrete materials.

- Plan for regular, short sessions practising vocabulary and use chanting, singing or actions to aid learning and remembering. Provide illustrated science dictionary sheets for class use. Provide and encourage the use of reference charts, diagrams and concrete materials and give them an acceptable status by making them available for all to use.
- Use pupil reminder books where examples of particular science vocabulary with a personal explanation/pictogram are noted.
- Aim for a multi-sensory teaching/learning style.
- Remember there may be difficulties with understanding verbal explanations and instructions and this may affect investigation work. Pupils may need lots of demonstration and supervised practice in working out what to do to tackle an investigation.
- Demonstrate and talk through how a decision has been reached.
- In literacy time practise reading for meaning with science investigations and encourage the pupils to expect the text to make sense. Teach the vocabulary involved, discuss which are the key words/parts of the problem and what the pupil has to do, and highlight the important parts. Use concrete apparatus if needed. When finished, help the pupil to talk through what they did.
- Some children will have particular difficulties with AT 1 where they are expected to hypothesize. We have found it helpful to break down the targets for AT 1 as detailed overleaf.
- Check written work frequently so that errors can be dealt with before they become learned as correct and while the pupil remembers the task. Provide frameworks for recording and use a variety of methods - highlighting, circling, matching, cutting and pasting given pictures.
- Allow adequate time for neat work and if necessary build in practice time, practising writing/drawing faster while maintaining neatness. Link this to investigative work - set up a fair test on adequate time for recording work.

In science, teachers can directly target vocabulary and concept work and build in lots of 'hands-on' experiences so that children with speech and language impairment can thoroughly enjoy the subject. Pupils will steadily become more confident with science vocabulary and straightforward knowledge, though they often need support with making sensible predictions and in generalizing their findings. It is necessary then to establish priorities for each pupil to ensure appropriate 'revisiting' and consolidation of knowledge and skills.

Experimental and Investigative

1	Beginning to recognize same and different.	Is interested, chooses to observe materials, displays.	Given a reminder, uses senses when observing.	Can answer closed questions. (Is it hot? Can it bend?)
	Can answer forced alternatives. (Is it rough or smooth?)	Can complete statements. (It isn't hard it's _______)	With help joins in simple discussion. Beginning to offer own ideas.	Draws simple charts to communicate ideas.
2	Chooses from given ideas of how an investigation should proceed.	Answers one-option questions. (Will this sink if I put it in the water?)	Answers How and What questions. (How does it move? What is it made of?)	Listens and selects likely ideas from given ones of 'What might happen if'
	Makes observations.	With some help uses own ideas.	Has used a range of simple equipment.	Records findings. Can say if they were expected.
3	Responds to suggestions of how to create an investigation.	Makes own suggestions of how to create an investigation.	Asks relevant questions. (How/Why/What will happen if?)	Makes predictions.
	Makes relevant observations. Uses a range of equipment, takes measurements.	With help will carry out fair test. Knows and can explain why it is fair.	Records in a variety of ways.	Can explain observations and any patterns found in measurements. Can say what they have found out from work.

Wider curriculum

6

As previously stated the general difficulties given at the start of this chapter apply to all areas of the curriculum. It is worth giving further thought to vocabulary, since when the whole curriculum is taken into consideration there is a wealth of vocabulary to be learned. It is essential to be realistic and set each child achievable aims in terms of the amount of vocabulary to be covered and, hopefully, remembered.

In history and geography the following is the vocabulary we target. However, we are aware that for some of our children this will not be consistently remembered or understood by the end of Key Stage 1.

History

Chronological awareness:

Can sequence a set of picture cards into a logical order. 2/ 3/ 4/ 5/ 6/ more			Can sequence a set of picture cards and give a spoken description or account of the event. 2/ 3/ 4/ 5/ 6/ more		
Can sequence and show understanding of:			Can show understanding and recall vocabulary for use:		
Yesterday	Today	Tomorrow	Today/ Yesterday/ Tomorrow	Days of the week	Months/A year/Years old/Age
What I have already done	What I am doing	What I'm going to do next	Seasons	Night/Day	Morning/ Afternoon/ Evening
This morning	This afternoon	This evening	Old/New	Old/Young	Clock times
When I was a baby	Now	When I grow up	Before/After/ Afterwards	Soon/Now/ Later/Then	Once/Often/ Usually
Old	New		Suddenly	Again	Sometimes/ Never
When Gran was little	When Mum was little	Now I'm little	While/Yet/ Until	Already/ Always	Almost/ Nearly
Long, long ago	Long ago	Now	Real/Imaginary	Alive/Dead	Adult, grown -up/Child

Geography

Shows understanding and can recall for use:

In/ on/ under/ behind/ in front/ up/ down/ over/ off/ out/ top/ bottom/ next to/ between/ against/ far/ near/ high/ low/ corner/ middle/ edge/ big/ little/ long/ short/ tall/ wide/ narrow/ thick/ thin/ deep/ shallow/ above/ below/ along/ forwards/ backwards/ sideways/ across/ through/ back/ front/ at/ to/ from/ about/ beside/ into/ out of/ together/ apart/ around/ towards/ away from/ inside/ outside/ anywhere/ everywhere/ nowhere/ somewhere/ here/ where/ there
Vocabulary connected with vehicles/ weather/ buildings/ jobs/ town and country

In **art, design, ICT, PE and music** we focus on providing as much enjoyable 'hands-on' experience as possible. The vocabulary we have prioritized in these subjects is included in our First Words list in Appendix 2. In this way overlearning is built in as this vocabulary is addressed in language work as well as specific curriculum tasks. This vocabulary has been carefully chosen but not designated to particular curriculum subjects since there are so many overlaps, e.g. position words could go under language, mathematics, PE, geography, music, art, design or ICT.

Some children with speech and language impairment have considerable success **learning a second language** but it has to be accepted that some find it very difficult. In Wrexham our children learn Welsh as a second language and it is my experience that many of them find it very difficult. So we limit the vocabulary and use it repeatedly with visual aids, role-play, songs and rhymes.

Questioning is used in all curriculum areas and it may be helpful to consider the nature of questions and their hierarchy of complexity (Appendix 4). The Guess Who game is particularly useful for developing questioning skills.

When considering the development of language, as mentioned above, **play and 'hands-on' activities** are essential. Play situations can be set up to teach particular vocabulary or language concepts. Play can be structured to reinforce or overlearn this language, then later the children will, hopefully, incorporate the same language in their own play.

Play can give an opportunity to relate language to something concrete; something that can be touched, seen, smelled and tasted, something that can be directly experienced. This ensures that language is used meaningfully, which is especially important for our children.

Play can lead to the exploration and development of particular manipulative skills, organizational skills, imagination and reading and writing skills. For instance, dressing and undressing dolls helps the children develop their own dressing skills, while role-play can develop a depth of understanding in topic work and allows for reading and writing with a purpose.

In specialist settings the children work intensively. Usually there is an adult on hand expecting a 'best try' and unless we plan carefully there is little 'down time'. 'Down time' is needed for the children to relax, to unwind a little and to recharge their batteries. The bonus is that during these times, through play and activities, they can be consolidating language work already covered in a more intense session.

Difficulties with language may have meant that some children were unable to derive much benefit or enjoyment from play; they may have missed out on some of the ordinary, day-to-day experiences and social development that occurs through play in the early years at home. Many of our young children with speech and language impairment have not participated in much play at all. As their language skills develop they need the opportunity to experience successful play situations they may have missed in earlier years.

Successful play encourages language development, and language and communication are an integral part of successful play.

7 Assessment

Recent research (Law *et al.*, 2000) shows that one in every ten children will experience some kind of speech and language impairment during their time in school. So in every class there are likely to be at least two or three children with varying degrees of speech and language difficulty. The severity of their difficulties may not warrant intensive support but may be interfering with their learning and affecting their behaviour. Identification and assessment is necessary to provide appropriate support and differentiation of the curriculum.

This chapter has been designed to assess the wide range of difficulties that constitute speech and language impairment. It is intended that the pupil's age and stage of development be taken into consideration and the assessment tasks be used selectively. Usually Early Years pupils would complete fewer tasks than a Year 1 or Year 2 pupil and junior age pupils would complete more. The tasks can be carried out through a mixture of one-to-one sessions and classroom activities. Most require careful observation and it is always useful to involve more than one person in such observation and carry this out over several weeks wherever possible.

This assessment chapter has been designed to be photocopiable and as flexible as possible, so that it can be used to meet individual assessment needs. The whole chapter may be copied for use or particular sections can be used as stand-alone assessments. If a pupil is having difficulties with listening and following instructions, for instance, then the Receptive Language tasks can be used. Similarly if a pupil is having difficulties at playtime or with social language then the Social Use of Language section and, perhaps, the Behaviour section can be used.

The assessment tasks are mostly self-explanatory - tick/circle statements as appropriate and record the pupil's responses for the exercises. For those sections where further explanation is required, notes are given. Please contact jillmcminn.public@bigfoot.com if you have any queries. Some children with SLI can be very difficult to understand and in this case the aim is to note whether any verbal responses were made and to attempt to write as much as possible of what was actually said. The vocabulary pictures will last longer if laminated and it is helpful to make an extra laminated copy of the sequencing pictures so they can be set out in order by the pupil. Summary sheets for the whole assessment are included.

Parents/carers are experts on their child and often have information that is not so readily available to professionals. Their information is vital to provide the 'whole picture' so you will also find a questionnaire for them. Some parents/carers may prefer to come in and talk through their contribution and have it noted down during the discussion. Others may prefer to write an account but, in our experience, many prefer to use a questionnaire as a guideline.

It is useful to obtain the pupil's view of their own learning, their successes and their difficulties – sheets for this are also provided.

The overall aim of this chapter is to provide a straightforward assessment tool that can help pinpoint particular speech and language impairments and provide relevant information that can, in turn, inform decision-making on appropriate support.

Notes of explanation

Medical

Hearing
Some children with SLI have fluctuating hearing loss that can be significantly and adversely affected by:

- illness
- colds
- chest infections
- ear infections
- the pollen count
- allergies.

Sight
Please note that some children with SLI may:

- have difficulties with focusing and tracking as distinct from distance vision;
- be highly distractible visually;
- be adversely affected by bright light, including sunlight and fluorescent lighting.

Part 1: Self-confidence, learning style and sociability, and Part 2: Play/involvement

Many pupils with SLI have low self-esteem and may have difficulties with attention. Social language difficulties and immaturity can significantly affect the development of play and self-help skills.

Involvement scale – This is a useful way of guiding observation on play and learning style.

Part 3: Expressive language

All the Expressive Language tasks are aimed at assessing *spoken* language.

Speech production difficulties

These can be noted down during one-to-one conversation, conversation with peers and group/class talk.

Listening to pairs of words and identifying if they are the same or different is a complex task but nonetheless it is useful to assess a pupil's ability to do this. It helps to complete several practice pairs first.

Multi-syllabic words

Many pupils with SLI have difficulty processing and producing the correct number of syllables in multi-syllabic words so even if their speech is difficult to understand or unintelligible noting down the number of syllables attempted by putting a dot for each is very useful.

Tapping rhythms

These exercises can be done during percussion sessions or on a table-top with an inverted pencil or by clapping hands. Tap the beats while saying the word, one beat for each syllable.

Ability to identify and imitate a range of sounds can be monitored during class percussion/music sessions and through using simple sound lotto games. Learning Materials Ltd, Dixon Street, Wolverhampton, WV2 2BX (www.learning.materials.btinternet.co.uk) has a range of special educational needs materials at reasonable prices, including sound lotto.

Vocabulary

Use the pictures given. The tasks can be carried out in three different ways if appropriate:

1. Ask the child to label each picture. ('Tell me what the boy is doing.' or 'Who is this?' or 'What colour?' 'Where is the . . .?')
2. Give the target word and ask the child to point to the matching picture. ('Point to *walk*?' or 'Show me the boy who is *walking*'.)
3. Give the target word in a sentence and ask the child to point to the matching picture.

Some children may have difficulty interpreting the pictures; but this in itself gives valuable information. However, you may wish to use more realistic photos or have other children show the action verbs to make this task more accessible.

Classifying and labelling

This task is like the vocabulary task but includes asking for the class or set name (people, vehicles, etc.).

Mathematics and science

Understanding mathematics and science vocabulary can be noted during mathematics and science sessions and/or assessed separately.

Grammar

Grammar difficulties can be noted down during one-to-one conversation, conversation with peers and group/class talk.

Part 4: Receptive language

Listening, identifying and remembering

Simple percussion instruments that make a significantly different sound are used for the first task. Percussion instruments that make a similar sound are used for the second task. The pupil needs to be blindfolded or simply facing away from the adult and the instruments.

Listening and repeating back

A significant number of children with SLI also have memory difficulties; these can be with short-term memory or immediate recall, working memory or retention of information *while* processing it and acting upon it or with long-term memory – storage of information for future use. These tasks are directed at short-term memory; however, if appropriate the remembering numbers task can be repeated and the child can be asked to repeat back the numbers in reverse order. This then addresses working memory skill.

Following instructions

When a child is said to be operating at a particular 'word level' this relates to the number of information-carrying words in sentence or utterance. The total number of words may be greater. In this task the information-carrying words are in bold.

Retelling a story

Allow the child to see the picture but mask the words as the idea is to remember rather than read the text.

Sequencing

The pictures and the baseboard will need to be prepared in advance. They will obviously last longer if they are laminated and work well if Velcro is used. Ask the child to look carefully at all the pictures then place them on the baseboard in the right order to tell the story. Record the order in which the child sequences the pictures by circling the correct number under each picture. Ask the child to tell the story ('Tell me the story' or 'What happens?'). Scribe what the child says as best you can; it can be useful to use a tape recorder and write it up later.

Part 5: Social use of language (pragmatics)

When you ask the child to cut the paper but don't provide any scissors, and ask the child to bring you the adhesive tape, you are finding out whether the child has any strategies to respond. Some children will quickly say, 'I can't, I've got no scissors' or 'What?' or 'I don't know what it is', but children with pragmatic difficulties are more likely to get up and wander around or sit and smile but do and say nothing. So you are noting the response and what strategies are in place.

Pupil information

Name ______________________________

Class/Year group ______________________________

Date of birth ______________________________

Age at assessment ______________________________

Medical information

Hearing

Sight

Other

7

Part 1: Self-confidence, learning style and sociability

Very restless, constantly distracted.	Can settle to task if closely supervised but easily distracted.	Settles to task but doesn't always complete.	Settles to task and completes with a minimum of distraction.	Settles well, works well, completes work.
Retiring and nervous, no self-confidence.	Hesitant and trusts self only in very familiar circumstances.	Not markedly nervous, confident in familiar circumstances.	Self-reliant, unruffled by new experiences.	Very self-reliant.
Easily discouraged.	Makes feeble attempts but soon discouraged.	Tackles easier tasks and fairly persistent with harder ones.	Persists despite difficulties.	Very persistent, undismayed by difficulties.
Separates calmly from parents/taxi escort.	Accepts new social situations, visits/visitors.	Indicates needs, toilet, thirst, help with task, pain.	Shows awareness of others' feelings. Shows concern for others.	Shows some understanding of social environment – sits quietly in service.
Shows understanding of humour, jokes.	Appropriate turn-taking skills.	Shows awareness of obvious hazards.	Uses appropriate greetings, volume.	Shows awareness of rules. Moves sensibly around school.
Accepts new social situations.	Understands the need for rules.	Is beginning to be able to make informed choices and decisions.	Can work co-operatively with others.	Shows awareness of safety and danger in a range of situations.
Can ask for help when necessary.	Understands that behaviour has consequences.	Takes responsibility for own actions.	Growing awareness of appropriate behaviour in a range of social situations.	

7

Part 2: Play/involvement

Approx 2.6 years	Avoids company, solitary.	Plays near others, watches them at play.	No idea of sharing/ turn-taking	Imitates domestic activities.	Plays with miniature toys meaningfully with running commentary.
Approx 3.0 years	Tries to join in, makes overtures to others.	Joins in play with others.	Understands sharing.	Likes to help with shopping, tidying.	Enjoys floor play with toys. Much make-believe play with objects/ people
Approx 4.0 years	Seeks company. Needs, seeks out company of other children.	Finds it hard to keep up with playtime games, language.	Is alternately co-operative and aggressive but understands need to argue with words not blows.	Generally more independent, can help when directed.	Floor games more complicated, favours role-play, dressing up.
Approx 5.0 years	Chooses own friends and whether to play alone or with others.	Co-operative in play situations. Friendly, good mixer.	Floor games very complicated, builds constructively.	Generally more sensible, understands need for tidiness though may need a reminder.	Flits from one activity to another. Can sustain play session.
5+ years	Makes friends. Understands what makes a good friend. Makes and maintains friendships.	Understands that people have different preferences, views and beliefs. Can resist negative peer pressure.	Shows concern for and helps others. Shows care and consideration, respects and values others.	Understands need for tidiness and order and is able to organize materials and activities. Is fair and honest and respects the property of others.	Can sustain interest in socializing and breaktime activities. Has a hobby or interest.

Involvement scale

Level 1	Level 2	Level 3	Level 4	Level 5
Frequently non-active	Sporadic activity	Usually engaged in some sort of activity	Usually active	Often shows involvement in activities
Absent-minded/ aimless	Occasionally doing puzzles, playing in water	Activity lacks intensity	Activity has real meaning	Continuously engaged in meaningful activities
Not really aware of what they are doing, not purposefully active	Daydreaming and messing around or dabbling	Performance is a succession of meaningless actions	Operates near boundaries of capacity	Easily makes choices
Appears to be involved but actions are stereotypical/ repetitive		Lack of energy	May need some support or stimulation	Not easily distracted
		Often easily distracted		Involvement is natural, intrinsic motivation
		Short attention span		Persistence, energy, complexity are generally present

Used with permission, from an article by Chris Rider (2002) 'Well-being and involvement' in *Special Children*, February/March, Questions Publishing.

7

Part 3: Expressive language

Speech quality

Speech is clear and intelligible

Yes	No

Speech is unintelligible

Some of the time	Most of the time	All of the time

Expression

Uses expression when speaking	Speaks in a monotone with no expression

Volume

Uses appropriate volume	Often shouts	Speaks very quietly

Response

Responds verbally to adults	Answers register
Responds verbally to peers	Joins in with rhymes and songs

Can:

smile	pout	blow	suck cheeks in	move tongue in and out	move tongue up and down	lick all round lips

Ask pupil to listen and say if the following pairs sound the same or different (practise pairs – man/man, rain/rain, hat/house, cat/cot):

Adult says: Pupil says:

Adult says		Pupil says	
ten	ten	same	different
sun	fun	same	different
bar	bar	same	different
cot	got	same	different
lab	lap	same	different
red	red	same	different
mat	met	same	different
pot	pit	same	different

7

Multi-syllabic

Omits syllables from multi-syllabic words (getti for spaghetti, benture for adventure)

Give examples:

____

____

____

____

Repeating multi-syllabic words (if unintelligible put a dot for each syllable attempted):

biscuits	helicopter
after	television
Tesco	machinery
butterfly	refrigerator
adventure	immediately
forgotten	imagination

Rhythm

Tapping/clapping rhythms:

dog *	hat *	girl *	table * *	yellow * *
banana * * *	sausages * * *	television * * * *	refrigerator * * * * *	

Can identify/Can imitate:

common everyday sounds
high/low sounds
loud/quiet sounds
long/short sounds

Rhyme

Adult says each, child identifies the rhyming pair

7

Give a rhyme for:

bee
sheep
rocket

Alphabet (see Word Banks, Appendix 5)

Can sing/say it Yes/No
Can give initial sound as adult says 'arrow begins with …'

On hearing the word can give the first sound, the last sound and the middle sound

bat	got	tell		
map	duck	sad		
can	pet	big	got	sun

Can blend (tell me which word I am sounding out)

i...t	n. . .o	m...a...n	p...i. . .g	f. . .r. . .o. . .g	b. . .l. . .e. . .d	ch. . .i. . .n

Can spell out/decode

cab	vet	jig	fox	sun	shop	chat	thin	queen	king	blot	bran	clip	crab

flan	frog	glad	grin	plop	pram	trip	twin	slip	scat	skid	smut	snug

swim	rain	yard	seek	fern	pies	goat	zoo	look	soil	fork	loud

buzz	mane	kite	rode	tune

7

Vocabulary

Colours
Use crayons or felt pens and ask 'what colour?' or 'what colour is this?'

red	orange	yellow	green	blue	black	white
brown	pink	purple	grey	gold	silver	
dark/light	What colours mix together to make pink?		What colours mix together to make purple?			

Verbs

Recognizes picture and can label (see pictures on page 94):

walk	sit	sleep	wake up	eat	drink
sing	read	blow nose	wash	comb	wave

Adjectives

Recognizes object and can label (see pictures, page 97):

big/little	happy/sad	hot/cold	open/closed

Positions

Recognises picture and can label:

in	on	under	behind	in front	between

Class terms

Classifying and labelling – recognizes picture, can label, put into correct set and give the name of the set (see pictures, pages 95–97):

Furniture	chair	chest of drawers	bed
Vehicles	plane	boat	bike
People/Family	mum	dad	boy
Tools	brush	scissors	pencil
Drink	tea/coffee	water	
Jobs	postman	fireman	nurse
Food	apple	eggs	cake
Animals	dog	giraffe	horse
Clothes	coat	shoes	scarf
Weather	rain	sun	snow
Buildings	house	school	castle

Mathematics and science

Can answer closed questions:	Can answer forced alternatives:	Can complete statements:
Is a feather heavy?	Is your pencil longer or shorter than mine?	A feather isn't heavy it's ________
Have you got more?	Are you taller or shorter than …?	We eat breakfast in the ________
Is ice cream hot?	Is an apple rough or smooth?	A cushion isn't hard it's ________
Can a pencil bend?	Is a cheese grater rough or smooth?	The table isn't rough it's ________

Can show understanding of:

wet/dry	hard/soft	rough/smooth

7

Using counters and/or shapes:

Same/different:	More/less:
Shape	How many more?
Pattern	How many less?
Amount	

Same and different

Use toy animals and if necessary prompt on colour, size, shape, home, sound, etc. For older children use scissors and knife.

	Same/Different	Comments
Cow and horse		
Scissors and knife		

Conversation

Attempt a conversation about toys the child likes to play with or food likes/dislikes.

Grammar

Uses in conversation and directed group/class work:

Determiners (the/a)	(Can I go to **the** toilet?) (She's got **a** toy.)	Yes	No
Correct tenses (regular and irregular)	Present (he is running/ he's running, he is playing) Past (she went out, she ran)	Yes	No
Plurals	Regular (cars, dogs, trees) Irregular (mice, fish, people)	Yes	No
Pronouns	(I me my mine you your yours he she it they we)	Yes	No
Possessives	(Ann's coat, his coat, her coat, their coats, our coats, his, hers, theirs, ours)	Yes	No
Questions (What, Where, Who)	(What is it? Where's Jenny? Who is that? Which one? When is it playtime? How does that work? Why does this happen? What would happen if...?)	Yes	No

7

Answering questions

Younger children

What do you cut with?		
What do you drink from?		
Give the opposite of sad fast		
Who lives in your house?		
Where do you live?		
What pets have you got?		
Are you a boy or a girl?		
Is it hot or cold today?		
Where is the sun? What is it like?		
Who goes in a fire engine? What do firemen do?		
Cake is food ... cars are ...		
Tell me two vehicles drinks		
What do you do first of all in the morning?		
Is it morning or afternoon?		

Older children

Can you tell me four different things you cut with?		
What do you drink lemonade from? What do you drink tea from?		
Give the opposite of miserable short		
What's your address and who lives in your house?		
Have you got a pet? If you could have a/another pet what would you have?		
Are you male or female?		
What's the temperature today?		
What is the sun like? Why is it important? What would happen if there was no sun?		
What is the same and what is different about a fire officer and a police officer?		
Cake is food ... cars are ...		
Tell me two breakfast foods Tell me two ocean vehicles		
Is it morning or afternoon?		
Can you tell me what you do through the day – start with first thing in the morning.		

7

Part 4: Receptive language

Listening

Shows good listening behaviours at: Story time Group work Class input

Very fidgety and easily distracted, doesn't easily engage: Story time Group work Class input

Can show has listened and understood by responding to simple questions and straightforward directions.

Attention

Pays fleeting attention Highly distractible	Needs much coaxing and support to start a task	Will attend to own choice of task for a time Finds it difficult to ignore other stimuli	Will attend to own or adult-given task Can't tolerate interruptions, must stop to listen then start activity	Integrated attention for short spells, copes with interruptions Can listen while carrying on activity Externalizes language	Sustained, controlled, integrated attention Internalizes language

Listening, identifying and remembering

Correctly identified Drum Claves Bells

Correctly identified (Similar sound) Marraccas Red shaker

With eyes closed can listen and recall by playing back in the correct order

2 3 4 5 percussion sounds

Listening and repeating back numbers

(two digits – 3 years) (three digits – 4 years) (four digits – 5 years) (five digits – 6/7 years)

1	4		3	5		2	6

2	5	3		1	3	2		4	2	5

1	4	3	5		2	4	2	5		3	1	4	4

1	7	2	5	9		8	6	4	2	5		9	7	5	3	1

If the pupil is very good at repeating back ask the pupil to *reverse* the numbers, e.g. the adult says 17259 and the pupil has to say 95271.

Pupil managed to recall and say in reverse order:

1	4		3	5		2	6

2	5	3		1	3	2		4	2	5

1	4	3	5		2	4	2	5		3	1	4	4

1	7	2	5	9		8	6	4	2	5		9	7	5	3	1

Repeating sentences

House	and	tree											
He	is	a	man										
The	bird	got	a	worm									
The	man	went	under	a	car								
My	brown	dog	likes	to	go	upstairs							
The	boat	out	there	is	going	up	and	down					
My	Mum	is	going	to	the	supermarket	and	then	to	see	my	Nan	

When	I	go	to	football	with	my	Dad	we	always	wear	our	football	scarves
and	we	cheer	and	jump	up	when	they	score					

Following instructions

Touch red (two-word level)		**Go** and **touch** a **door** then **sit down** (five-word level)	
Kneel behind the **chair** (three-word level)		**Touch something red then touch metal.** (six-word level)	
Stand between the **chair** and the **table** (four-word level)		**Point to something** we **cut with then stand in front** of the **chair.** (seven-word level)	

Retelling a story

Tell the pupil the story and ask them to retell it from memory:

One day Abby (**1**) was going to the shop (**2**) and she saw a dog (**3**) going on the busy road (**4**). She ran and picked him up (**5**) and looked at his collar (**6**) for his name (**7**). His name was Spot (**8**). Abby took Spot to the police station (**9**). The policeman said, 'I'll look after Spot until his owner comes.' (**10**)

Details recalled									
1	2	3	4	5	6	7	8	9	10

Details remembered after questioning									
1	2	3	4	5	6	7	8	9	10

Retelling a story 2

Tell the pupil the story and ask them to retell it from memory:

One morning Ben's Mum went to the shop. 'I won't be long,' she said. Ben went outside to play football and the door blew shut behind him. He could not get back in the house. He decided to play football in the garden and wait for his Mum to get back. Then it started to pour with rain. Oh no! What could Ben do now?

Checklist for recall:

Correct sequence, main ideas, recall characters/details, can discuss and give opinions
Correct sequence, main ideas, recall characters, some details
Correct sequence, main ideas, recall characters, little detail
Some facts sequenced correctly, some characters, one/two details
Confused, unable to give gist, maybe one/two characters

Sequencing

Comments on approach/strategies

7

Part 5: Social use of language (pragmatics)

Greeting/eye contact

Responds to adult/peer greeting	Doesn't respond to adult/peer greeting Ignores and walks past Makes eye contact but doesn't respond
Uses appropriate eye contact	Doesn't use appropriate eye contact Looks at the floor but appears to be listening Is distracted and looking elsewhere
Uses appropriate stance/position	Doesn't use appropriate stance/position Stands too close, invading your personal space Addresses others from a distance without making it clear who they are talking to
Uses appropriate speech style	Doesn't use appropriate speech style Too loud Too formal Too informal Too monotonous
Uses 'good listening' rules Good sitting Good looking Good waiting Taking turns Good thinking Good joining in	Doesn't use 'good listening' rules Fidgets Is highly distractible Interrupts Talks about subjects other than the one under discussion Is hard to engage in discussion/joint activities
Initiates conversations, Volunteers information Makes appropriate comments with peers and/or with adults	Doesn't Is predominantly silent Has a range of avoidance strategies – toilet, crying, talking about a particular subject Talks but it is 'off the subject' Talks but starts in the middle of the subject and does not give enough information for easy conversation

Facial expression/gesture

Uses/responds to a range of facial expressions and gestures	Doesn't use/respond to a range of facial expressions and gestures Misinterprets a range of facial expressions and gestures
Says and shows how he/she feels	Doesn't, rarely shows emotion Has a blank/hard to read expression
Asks for help appropriately	Doesn't Asks but doesn't give enough information Gets upset Asks repeatedly about the same difficulty
Joins in fun and games, laughs appropriately	Doesn't join in Actively dislikes fun and games Laughs at things others don't find funny
Understands indirect requests e.g. Would you like to wash your hands now?	Doesn't understand indirect requests

7

Sabotaged requests

Ask child to cut paper **but don't provide scissors.**	
Ask child to get the **adhesive tape.**	

What am I?

I am in a room with a cooker, a sink and pots and pans. Where am I?	
I am a big animal, I give you milk. What am I?	
I call at your house and ask you to come out to play. Who am I?	
I am in an ambulance. Who am I? (Several possible answers)	

What goes together?

dog	pencil ....
boy	purse ....

Semantic links

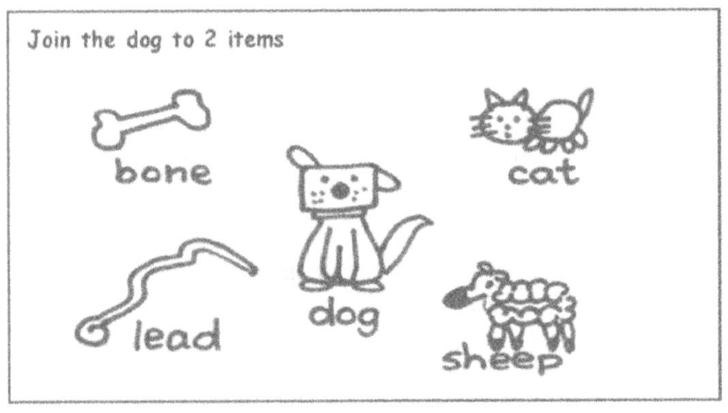

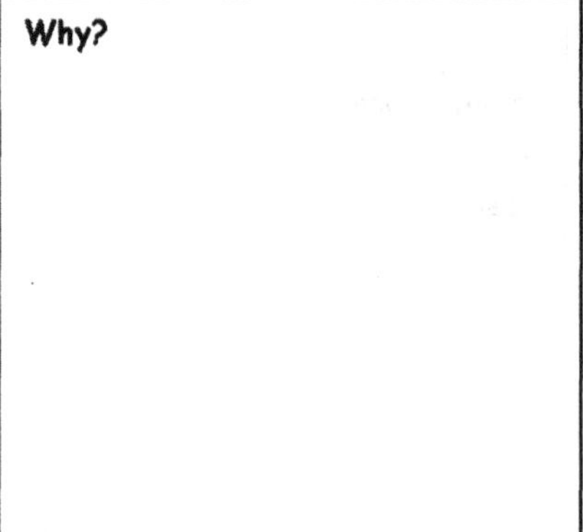

7

What's wrong?

What's wrong in these pictures?

There is something wrong in these pictures. Can you see what it is?

1 Man with a bucket on his foot	2 Wet pans and cutlery on the line	3 Cat skipping
Pupil points Pupil says	Pupil points Pupil says	Pupil points Pupil says

What's wrong in these sentences?

When it is cold we need gloves, scarves, swimming costumes and hats.	Gave correct response (swimming costumes)
At bedtime we need pyjamas, slippers, crayons and a toothbrush.	Gave correct response (crayons)
The dentist said, 'Open wide', and Sam got up and opened the door.	Gave correct response (Sam should have opened his mouth)

Part 6: Behaviour

Has difficulty socializing at playtimes	Has difficulty with fast-paced playground language and rules of games	Walks around alone or with adult	Often involved in difficulties

Examples of behaviour that causes concern

What happened	Circumstances surrounding incident – what happened before and afterwards	Possible misunderstandings of language or social language and expected behaviours

7

Part 7: Developmental Co-ordination Skills

Whole body movement and skills

Approx. 3 years	Can put on own shoes	Can walk forwards, backwards, sideways	Can catch a large ball thrown by an adult	Can walk on tiptoe	Can sit cross-legged and rise from kneeling not using hands
Approx. 3.6 years	Balances standing on one foot for two seconds	Can jump, jumps off a step both feet together	Can run with some control	Can walk on toes, heels	Cross lateral crawling
Approx. 4 years	Balances standing on one foot for three to five seconds	Walks up steps alternating feet	Can run fast Can catch a small ball thrown by adult	Can march in time to music	Can hop on preferred foot
Approx. 5 years	Balances standing on one foot for eight to ten seconds	Walks easily, with control along narrow line	Can run and stop with control Can throw and catch a ball	Can skip on alternate feet	Can climb wall bars
Approx. 6 years	Cross lateral movements L elbow to R knee R elbow to L knee ...	Can walk along off-ground balance bar with some support	Can smoothly run up and kick ball Can dribble and stop ball with foot	Can hit stationary ball with bat	Can bounce and catch ball
Approx. 7 years	Can hold steady balance for some time	Can jump over 25cm stick/rope	Can run, dodge, freeze with control	Can hit thrown ball with bat	Can skip with a rope

7

Self-help skills

Approx. 3 years	Can give first/full name on request. Knows own sex. Feeds self but spills some. Uses spoon and fork. Attends to toilet needs, may need help with buttons. Can undo buttons. Washes hands, may need help drying them.
Approx. 4 years	Eats skilfully with spoon and fork. Attends to own toilet needs. Can undress except for laces, back buttons, ties. Puts on socks, shoes, fastens some buttons. Washes, dries hands with some supervision.
Approx. 5 years	Can give name, age, address. Uses knife and fork well. Attends to own toilet needs and washes, dries hands. Can fasten buckles. Manages own coat.
5 years +	Can give name, age, address and other personal details. Manages washing, dressing, toilet and all personal hygiene well. Can organize own possessions and understands the need for order and tidiness.

Manipulative skills

Threading/paper folding			
Can thread five large beads (Approx. 3 years)	Can thread five small beads (Approx. 4 years)	Can fold 10cm piece of paper in two	Can fold 10cm piece of paper in quarters

Jigsaws			
Can complete a simple formboard (2.6 years)	Can complete a five-to ten-piece jigsaw	Can complete a 20- 50- 100 piece jigsaw	Uses good strategies, sorting, colour matching, picture matching

Scissor control				
Can snip (3 years)	Can cut roughly across paper (4 years)	Can cut roughly along line (4 years)	Can cut well along line, roughly round shapes (4.6 years)	Can cut well around shapes Can cut card and fabric

Crayoning			
Scribble crayoning (2.6 years)	Crayoning roughly (3 years)	Neatly with control (4.6 years)	Well, selecting appropriate colours (5 years)

7

Pencil control				
Holds pencil well (4 years)	Holding pencil ready to write can execute a 'frogs' legs' movement	Using one hand at a time can press each finger in turn to tip of thumb	Holding hands in front of chest can move fingers apart and together smoothly	Holding palm and fingers flat and straight can execute a wrist rotation in either direction

Can complete dot to dot Can complete a pencil maze	Can write over Can write under Can write	Can draw a recognizable: person (4 years) house (4 years)	Can write first name Can write full name

Copying shapes

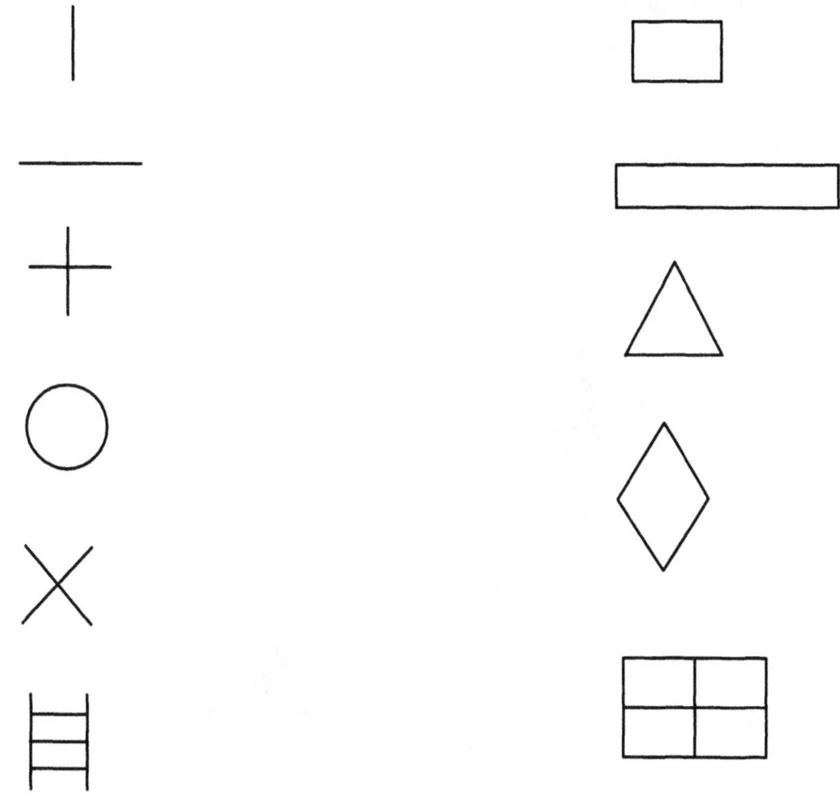

(3 years)	(4 years)	(5 years)	(6 years)	(7 years)

7

Part 8: Sensory integration difficulties

Visual problems With tracking, shifting gaze, e.g. from blackboard to paper on table and with interpreting by looking.
Hearing problems With locating sounds, identifying and discriminating between sounds.
Problems with taste and smell With over- or under-reaction to particular tastes and smells, leading to restricted diet and dislike of 'hands-on' activities.
Tactile problems With over- or under-reaction to touch, dislike of hair or nails being cut, lack of awareness of nose running or food spilled on clothes, fiddling with everything.
Vestibular and proprioceptive problems Difficulties with balance and body awareness.

Pictures for use during the assessment

Verbs

7

Classifying and labelling

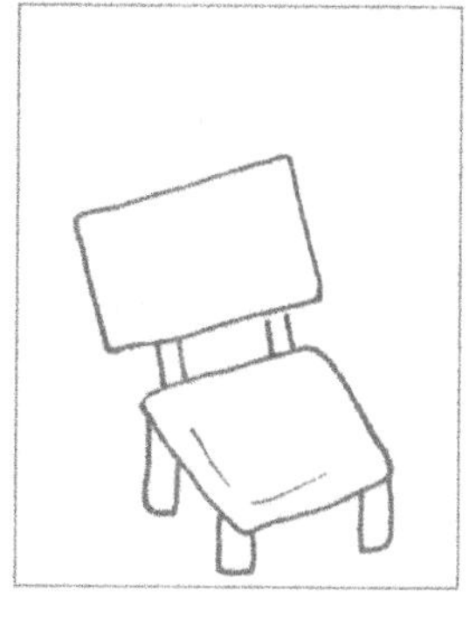

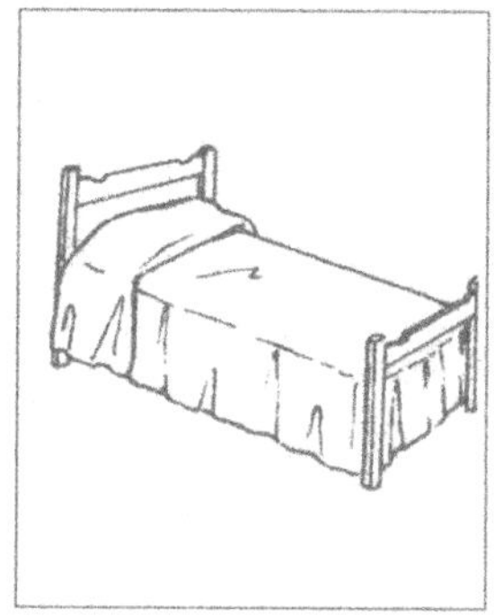

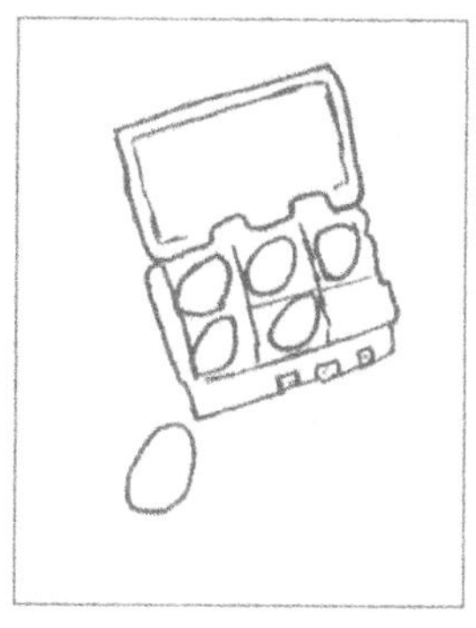

Classifying and labelling

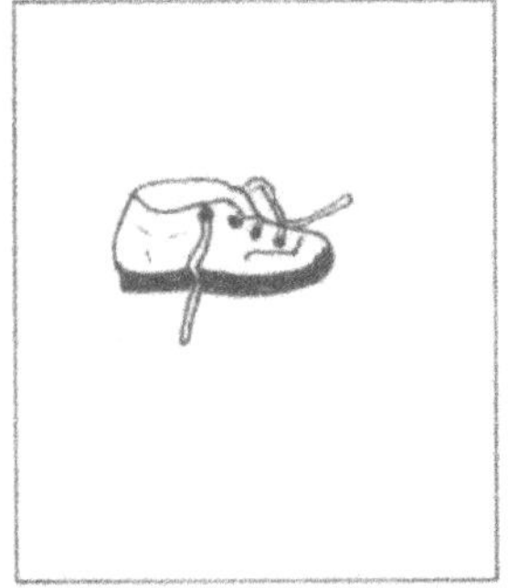

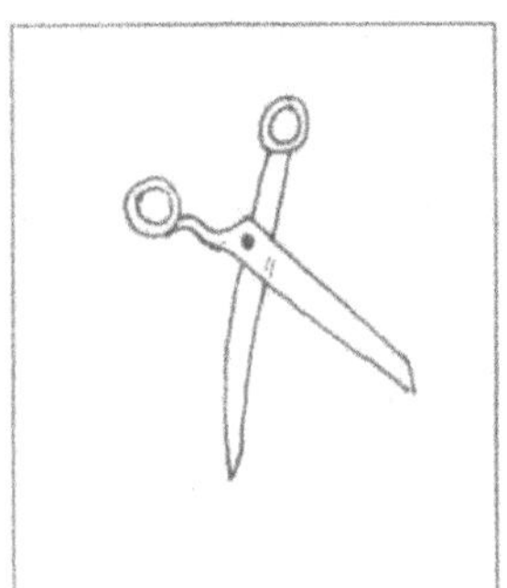

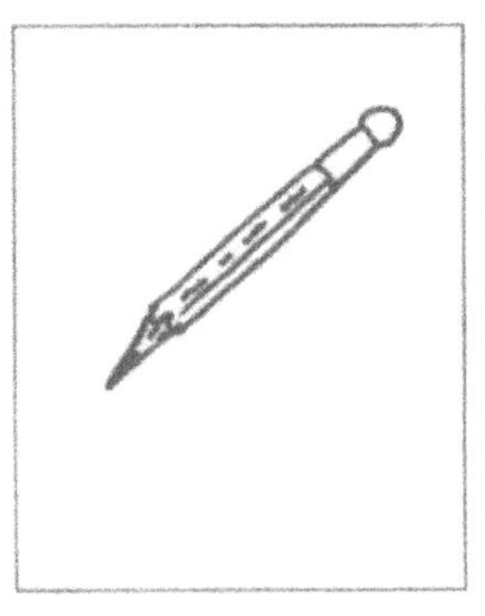

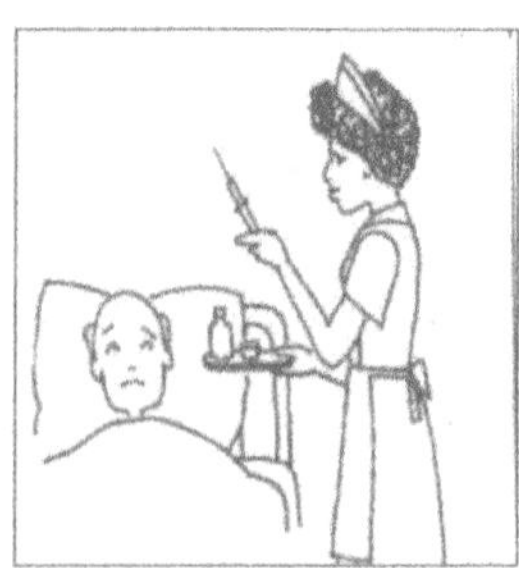

7

Hot/cold

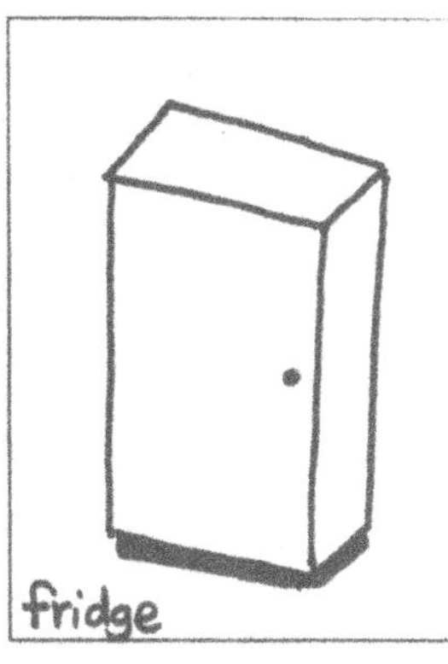

hot

cold

Open/closed

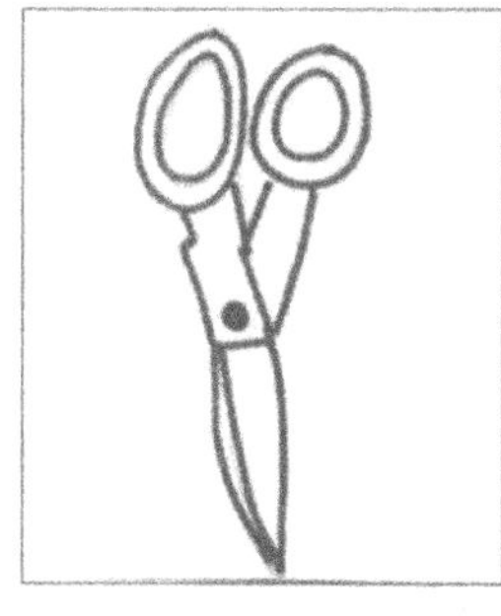

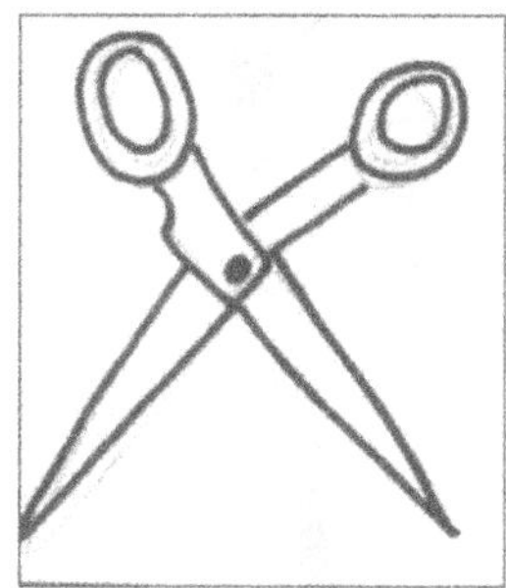

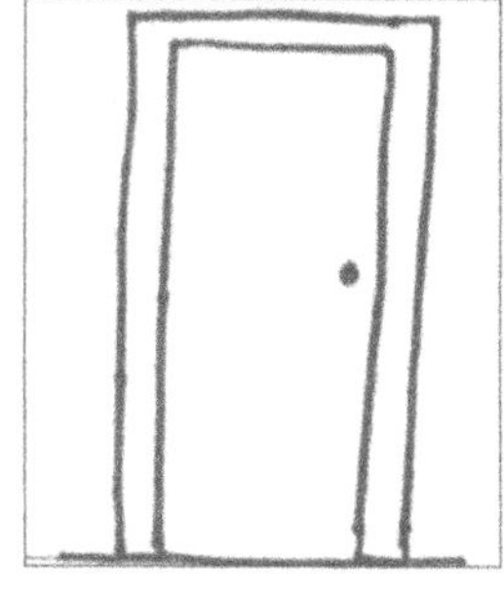

Summary sheet following assessment and observation

Name	DOB	Age at time of assessment

Task/Observation		Performance	Comments/IEP targets
Medical			
Self-confidence, learning style, sociability			
Play/involvement			
Expressive language			
Speech quality			
Multi-syllabic			
Rhythm			
Rhyme			
Alphabet			
Blending			
Decoding			
Vocabulary	Colours		
	Verbs		
	Adjectives		
	Positions		
	Class terms		
Mathematics and science			
Same and different			
Conversation			
Grammar	Determiners		
	Tenses		
	Plurals		
	Pronouns		
	Possessives		
	Questions		
Answering questions			

Receptive language			
Listening			
Attention			
Listening, identifying and remembering			
Listening and repeating back numbers			
Repeating sentences			
Following instructions			
Retelling a story			
Sequencing			
Social use of language			
Greeting/Eye contact			
Facial expression/Gesture			
Sabotaged requests			
What am I?			
What goes together?			
What's wrong?			
Behaviour			
Behaviour			
Developmental co-ordination skills			
Whole-body movement and skills			
Self-help skills			
Manipulative skills	Threading/Paper folding		
	Jigsaws		
	Scissor control		
	Crayoning		
	Pencil control		
	Copying shapes		
Sensory integration difficulties			
Visual			
Hearing			
Taste and smell			
Tactile			
Vestibular and proprioceptive			

Parent questionnaire

[You may wish to use large print, double spacing and an easy-to-read font like comic sans when designing your letter and questionnaire for parents.]

Dear Parent

You are the person who knows your child best and it would be very helpful if you would tell us about your child. The form below is one way of doing this but if you'd prefer to write in your own words or you'd prefer to come in and talk it through with us please do so.

Share anything that has concerned you or continues to concern you as well as anything that has surprised or pleased you.

Full name of your child ____________________

What your child is usually called by family and friends ____________________

Position in family ____________________

What your child calls family members (grandparents, pets, sisters/brothers ...) and friends ____________________

When your child was a baby or very young – when and what you noticed that made you concerned (late to talk, walk, etc.)	
General health Eating and sleeping habits General fitness/tiredness Minor ailments Serious illnesses/accidents Medicines/special diet Absences from school	
Physical skills Crawling, running, jumping, etc. Riding a bike Colouring, drawing, writing, cutting Using construction kits or building blocks	
Self-help Washing, cleaning teeth, toileting, feeding, dressing General organization and independence	
Communication Can family understand your child's speech? Can less well-known people understand your child's speech?	

Communication continued	
Can your child tell what he/she wants? Can your child say more than one word? Does your child use more that one word? Use gestures? Understand when you ask your child simple things? Does your child ask for help if not understanding? Start and/or join in conversation? Describe? Explain? Can take and deliver a message? Use telephone? Anything else:	
Playing and socializing Uses imaginative play Likes listening to stories Plays well with siblings Plays well with others, Can take turns Enjoys going to parties Goes to playgroup happily Enjoys clubs/sports activities Mixes well or is a loner If left with known sitter accepts parental absence	
Behaviour Co-operates, shares Helps around the house Fits in with family routines Moods?	
Things your child does well	
Things your child finds difficult	
Concerns and worries you have about your child now and in the future	
What you think will help your child, what your child needs	
Anything else you wish us to know	

7

Pupil questionnaire

My name is ______________________________

I am __________ years old

In school I like

I find it hard to

I think I need some help with

talking	listening	making friends	behaving acceptably
moving and balancing		planning and organizing	my senses

How I feel about needing help

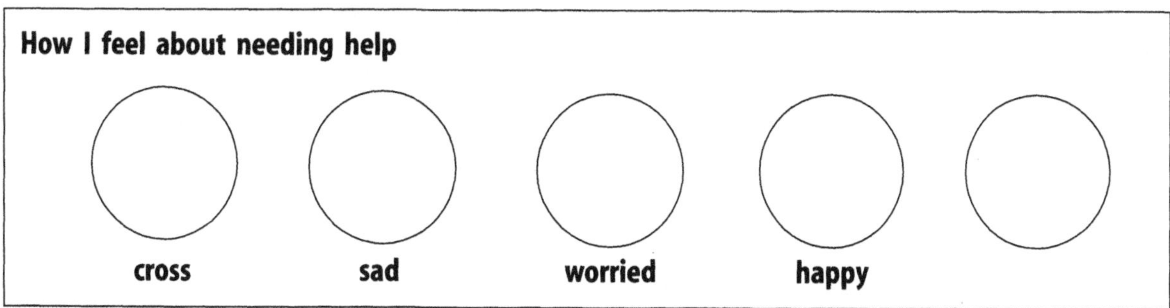

I want to be able to ...

I want to say ...

7

Sample summary sheets following assessment and observation

Pupil profile:
Tilly is aged 5½ and has been in a Reception class of 30 pupils in a mainstream school for one and a half terms. She is a very quiet child who seldom speaks, she rarely responds to adults and doesn't answer the register but has been heard talking with the other children in her class. Her speech is very difficult to understand. She seems to have difficulty remembering in a range of contexts, e.g. when reciting or singing nursery rhymes she does not join in and even on her own with the teacher seems not to know the words and in number games does not seem to remember the numbers. Nor does she remember the names of her teachers.

Tilly was assessed using the exercises provided in this book and the findings are summarized below. Her parents filled in a questionnaire and an attempt was made to record Tilly's feelings using the child questionnaire.

Name Tilly Jones	**DOB** 28 October 2000	**Age at time of assessment** 5½ years

Task/Observation	**Performance**	**Comments/IEP targets**
Medical	She has fluctuating hearing loss which is worse in the winter. She had grommets fitted when she was 4 but these are no longer in place.	Refer to Audiology Department at the hospital.
Self-confidence, learning style, sociability	She can settle to tasks but needs close supervision, needs help often to complete and is very easily distracted.	1:1 support or small group support to start with then gradually encourage more independent working using short achievable tasks.
Play/involvement	She plays near the other children, tries to join in, makes overtures but often ends up on the sidelines watching. She finds it particularly hard to join in and 'keep up' at playtime. Involvement scale level 2.	Support at playtime outside. Teach her the ring games the whole school knows. Help her 'find a friend'.
Expressive language		
Speech quality	Speech is unintelligible most of the time, she speaks very quietly or not at all. She has difficulty moving her tongue in different ways.	Liaise with speech and language therapy; if she has not been assessed enter her for an assessment.
Multi-syllabic	It was impossible to tell if she is including all syllables though she seemed to be giving the right number of sounds/noises for 2 syllable words only and gave 1 or 2 sounds/noises for all the others too.	

7

Rhythm		She made 1 beat for all the words. She could show understanding by identifying the correct picture for a range of common sounds.	Include some syllable tapping with and without percussion using: class-room vocabulary (can I go to the toilet or toilet please, I've finished, etc.), target vocabulary (food), class names.
Rhyme		She showed no understanding of rhyme.	Point out and stress in nursery and other rhymes and encourage her to join in with these. Play fill the gap games, e.g. Jack and Jill went up the _______ or Jack and Fred went off to ______, etc.
Vocabulary	Colours	She knew 5 colours.	Teach colours, this sometimes takes longer with children with SLI so may need to be a short daily task. Ask parents and family to help.
	Verbs	She showed understanding of a range of common vocabulary but has no group terms and wet/dry but not hard/soft, rough/smooth.	
	Adjectives		
	Positions		
	Class terms		
Mathematics and science		She showed no understanding of shape, pattern or any of this mathematics terminology.	Teach shape, this sometimes takes longer with children with SLI so may need to be a short daily task. Ask parents and family to help.
Same and different		Showed no understanding.	Use this vocabulary and work towards understanding in a range of class/ curriculum tasks, e.g. with shape make patterns that are the same and patterns that are different, during daily calendar work recall yesterday's weather and say whether it is the same or different as today's weather, etc.
Conversation		Very difficult but attempted a conversation about her family which was impossible to follow, so then we used pictures of animals and we talked about dogs. She has a dog at home but I couldn't tell what it was called. She didn't initiate any talk but did respond to my comments or questions but it was very difficult to understand what she said.	When working 1:1 try to have a short conversation about a known/shared context, e.g. play that she has just engaged in or PE that has just been carried out. Ask parents to help with this and tell you what she has done at home and encourage them to draw a simple picture that Tilly can use to help her to talk.

7

Receptive language		
Listening	Good listening and looking at the book in story time, she loves stories. Very fidgety in group or class sessions. She finds it difficult to ignore noises in class and is often distracted, then finds it hard to refocus.	Teach the whole class the good listening rules.
Attention		
Listening, identifying and remembering		
Listening and repeating back numbers	2 numbers	
Repeating sentences	2 words Identified all percussion but could only play back 2 sounds heard with eyes closed and not in right order.	
Following instructions	2-word level	Be aware and raise staff awareness of her level of understanding. Simplify instructions, give demonstrations and offer support where it is needed. Possibly include some 1:1 sessions.
Retelling a story	1 fact recalled 1 more after questioning	
Sequencing	Haphazard and single-word description – which was hard to understand.	Include sequencing of regular tasks and events into class carpet time, have pictures or symbols for these wherever possible, e.g. days of the week, lessons throughout the day, meals, etc.
Developmental co-ordination skills		
Whole-body movement and skills	From the parents' questionnaire it seems that Tilly may have some co-ordination difficulties.	Have 10 minutes a day practising these skills 1:1 or a small group or the class. Have a 'hand gym' bag or box in class with a range of manipulative tasks, e.g. spinners, pegs, plasticine, and direct Tilly to complete 2 tasks a day.

Sample Parent Questionnaire

Dear Parent

You are the person who knows your child best and it would be very helpful if you would tell us about your child. The form below is one way of doing this but if you'd prefer to write in your own words or you'd prefer to come in and talk it through with us please do so.

Share anything that has concerned you or continues to concern you as well as anything that has surprised or pleased you.

Full name of your child Tilly Jones

What your child is usually called by family and friends Tilly or Till

Position in family Oldest of 2, younger sister Jane

What your child calls family members (grandparents, pets, sisters/brothers . . .) and friends
Mum, Da (Dad), Ay (Jane), Gaga (Granny), Bob (Bob the dog)

When your child was a baby or very young – when and what did you notice that made you concerned (late to talk, walk, etc.)	Late to walk, talked at around 15 months but babbling
General health Eating and sleeping habits General fitness/tiredness Minor ailments Serious illnesses/accidents Medicines/special diet Absences from school	She had grommets fitted at 4 but they fell out and the doctor said she didn't need them any more
Physical skills Crawling, running, jumping, etc. Riding a bike Colouring, drawing, writing, cutting Using construction kits or building blocks	She can't ride her bike yet She loves stories and colouring
Self-help Washing, cleaning teeth, toileting, feeding, dressing General organization and independence	She needs help with these and is in nappies at night still – I am worried about this
Communication Can family understand your child's speech? Can less well-known people understand your child's speech? Can your child tell you what he/she wants? Can your child say more than one word? Does your child use more than one word? Use gestures? Understand when you ask your child simple things?	Me and her dad can usually make out what she wants but not from what she says as we can't understand that. She takes you to what she wants or points Sometimes she really cries and screams cos we don't know what she wants – it's awful

7

Does your child ask for help if not understanding? Starts and/or joins in conversation? Describe? Explain? Can take and deliver a message? Use telephone? Anything else:	
Playing and socializing Uses imaginative play Likes listening to stories Plays well with siblings Plays well with others, Can take turns Enjoys going to parties Goes to playgroup happily Enjoys clubs/sports activities Mixes well or is a loner If left with known sitter accepts parental absence	She plays by herself with her colouring and her doll She hates parties and won't stay without me
Behaviour Co-operates, shares Helps around the house Fits in with family routines Moods?	She is mostly OK but can be in a rage if you don't understand her
Things your child does well	She is gentle with her little sister and her Gran
Things your child finds difficult	Dressing, washing, going to the toilet – wiping herself – talking
Concerns and worries you have about your child now and in the future	Will she ever be able to talk better and get on in school?
What you think will help your child, what your child needs	I want someone to help her talk better
Anything else you wish us to know	

Sample Pupil Questionnaire

My name is Tilly

I am 4 **years old**

In school I like
Dolls

I find it hard to
Talk [prompted answer]

I think I need some help with

talking [prompted answer] **listening** **making friends** **behaving acceptably**

moving and balancing **planning and organising** **my senses**

How I feel about needing help

Cross

sad

worried

happy

I want to be able to ...
Skip [prompted answer]

I want to say ...
[Just shrugged]

8 Individual Educational Plans and Suggested Targets

Any pupil at School Action (SA) or School Action Plus (SAP) should have an individual educational plan (IEP). This is the detailed planning document of differentiated teaching and learning needed to support the pupil in achieving identified targets.

Targets need to be **SMART**:

- **S**pecific – when, where, how often, with whom. Are the targets specific to this pupil and linked to his/her assessment/annual review or statement?
- **M**easurable – this is the trickiest but the key one. When the target is written ask 'How will we all know if the target has been achieved?' When measuring you are looking for observable progress.
- **A**chievable/**A**ction words – prioritise and have only a few targets at any one time. Using action words helps to make the target achievable.
- **R**elevant/**R**ealistic – break down what you wish to achieve so that targets are written in small steps and pertain to the current situation and need.
- **T**imed – both as a measure, e.g. nine times out of ten or during carpet time four days out of five, as well as the overarching time, probably six to eight weeks/a half-term, by the end of which you expect no longer to need that particular target but to be setting the next one.

An IEP document needs to include:

- present level of performance
- a **few** targets
- strategies for support
- specific intervention details, resources and personnel involved.

To be most effective targets should be jointly planned by all involved professionals and parents and, wherever appropriate and possible, the pupil concerned. If there is no direct speech and language therapy involvement then it is important and helpful if advice from speech and language therapy services is sought.

A suggested format for the speech and language impairment IEP is given over the next few pages, beginning with a form to establish and record the present level of performance, a second form for current targets, and a third for the outcome of the target review meetings. There then follows a suggested format for setting out the targets. This includes columns for support, the environment, action statements, target and time. A range of targets is given below this table.

Individual educational plan – present level of performance

Initial referral sheet, to be completed by the teacher and then discussed with the parent

Name: Year: Date of Birth:
CoP Stage:

School: Class: Teacher:

Has speech and language impairment and has particular difficulties with (highlight the sentences below that apply):

Expressive language	**Receptive language**	**Social use of language**
• difficulty with clear, intelligible speech • difficulty with grammatical speech • difficulty with logical flowing speech • difficulty learning vocabulary	• difficulty following instructions • memory difficulties • difficulty understanding language	• difficulty relating to others • difficulty with social behaviours, codes • difficulty with fast-paced playground games • literal understanding and use of language

Sensory integration difficulties	**Developmental co-ordination difficulties (DCD)**	**Behaviour**
• visual problems with tracking, shifting gaze and interpreting by looking • hearing problems with locating sounds, identifying and discriminating between sounds • problems with taste and smell – over- or under-reaction to particular tastes and smells, leading to restricted diet and dislike of 'hands-on' activities • tactile problems – over- or under-reaction to touch, dislike of hair or nails being cut, lack of awareness of nose running or food spilled on clothes, fiddling with everything • vestibular and proprioceptive difficulties with balance and body awareness	• difficulties with whole body movements and balance • difficulties with manipulative skills • difficulties with organization and planning	• unacceptable behaviours • difficulty with focused attention, listening

Present level of performance of Expressive language, Receptive language, Social use of language, Sensory and co-ordination skills and behaviour (Teacher assessment or appropriate test scores)

8

Individual educational plan – current targets

Name: Year: Date of Birth: CoP Stage:

School: Class: Teacher:

Date	Target	Outside agencies involved	School staff involved	Resources	Date to be assessed	Progress made

Date of review meeting
Those to be invited
Signed Parent . . . . SENCo . . . . Class teacher . . . .
Pupil. . . . .

Individual educational plan – outcome of review

Name:	Year:	Date of Birth:	CoP Stage:
School:	Class:	Teacher:	

Outcome of review

School comments

Parents' comments

Pupil's comments

Outcome of review

Targets – suggested format

Select relevant and appropriate phrases from those given below.

Support	Learning environment	Can		Frequency	
Given a cued articulation sign visual support/reference a direct spoken prompt a multi-sensory cue (signed, visual, spoken) a model/demonstration repetition **Given a word-finding cue:** forced alternative first letter is it a long or a short word it sounds like it rhymes with description opposite **Given time** **Unaided**	1:1 In group class freer conversation Spontaneously	Respond appropriately Imitate Discriminate between Select Match Use/Produce Label/Say Identify/Demonstrate understanding by (pointing, touching, choosing, giving, saying) Say clearly/Pronounce Engage in/Join in Using known vocabulary, respond to Using known vocabulary, answer Using known vocabulary, give/complete By identifying and labelling in a range of tasks, show growing understanding of . . . By identifying and labelling in a range of tasks can show understanding of . . . Repeat back Recall/Remember Remember and deliver Listen and engage in Show has listened and understood by carrying out simple action instructions Sequence Sequence and retell By sensible response/behaviour, show growing understanding of . . . By sensible response/behaviour, show understanding of . . . Assert self appropriately	***Add in target statement from those possible targets given below**	[50, 75, 80 . . .] % [10, 15 . . .] minutes [4 out of 5 . . .] times By . . . [date] In [2] weeks Limited Sustained Automatically In directed session When observed answering When observed in freer conversation	of the session of the hour in the day in class throughout the day

8

Possible targets

Each target has been written to make best sense so includes the action words in brackets; choose the most appropriate words and phrases from the table above to suit your pupil and your situation.

Expressive language

General
[Can respond] verbally
[Can answer] register
[Can repeat] target language
[Can join in] rhymes, refrains, drama, role-play

Speech production
[Can imitate] tongue and lip movements accurately
[Can use] a straw to suck and to blow
[Can produce] a simple hand-clapped rhythm
[Can produce] common everyday sounds loud/quiet sounds long/short sounds high/low sounds
[Can produce] given sound/sounds [e.g. lip sounds /m/w/p/b/ etc]

Speech Therapy advice is recommended for these targets
[Can produce] multi-syllabic words (2 syllables) (3 syllables) (4 syllables) (5 syllables) (6 syllables)

Vocabulary

[Can produce] one-word labels (food, clothes, animals . . .)
[Can show understanding of] target vocabulary (e.g. food, clothes, animals . . .) or particular subject vocabulary (e.g. top, bottom, middle, first, next, last)
[Can answer] simple closed questions (Is it hot? Can it bend?)
[Can respond to] forced alternatives, key word last (Is it rough or smooth?) key word first (Is it smooth or rough?)
[Can finish] statements (It isn't hard it's ____ , Birds fly frogs ___)
[Can answer] one-option questions (Will this sink?)
[Can answer] more complex questions (What is it made from? Where does it live? Who did it? How does it move? When did it happen? Why . . . Because)

Grammar

8

[Can include] key words in the right order
[Can produce] two- three- four- five-word utterances
Can generate a sentence from given target vocabulary (e.g. given **rabbit** – a rabbit eats carrots or rabbits have long ears)
[Can produce] the correct pronoun (e.g. I, me, my, mine, you, your, yours, he, she, it, they, we)
[Can produce] the correct adverb (e.g. texture, sound, movement)

[Can produce] the correct adjective (e.g. quality, colour, texture, sound, shape, size)
[Can produce] the correct comparative (e.g. quality, colour, texture, sound, shape, size, movement)
[Can produce] the correct tense (   )
[Can produce] the correct plural (   )
[Can produce] the correct determiner (the, a)
[Can produce] the correct possessive (Mum's coat, Dad's coat, his coat, her coat)
[Can produce] the correct negative (don't, didn't, haven't, won't)
[Can produce] the correct abbreviation (I'm, we'd)
[Can produce] the correct conjunction (and, but, because, so, or, if . . .)
[Can use] simple, closed questions about an input
[Can use] the correct question (what, where, who, when, how, why)
[Can use] modal questions (Could you open a window?)
[Can use] reversed auxiliary questions (Is it cold?)

Sequencing

[Can sequence logically by giving] next picture/previous picture
[Can sequence logically by sorting] 2 3 4 5 6 pictures
[Can sequence logically by sorting] a given story (   ) facts out of ten
[Can give] correct sequence of events of familiar events (e.g. dressing, meals, etc.)
[Can recall] main ideas/characters/events of a familiar story
[Can recall] previous episodes of a serial story
[Can recall] a story giving some detail
[Can recall] a story giving an accurate, full retelling
[Can recall] a story relating characters and events to own experience
[Can listen] showing patience, tolerance, appreciation

Conversation

[Responds appropriately] to tone of voice
[Responds] verbally
[Answers] register
[Answers] in group situations
[Uses] appropriate volume
[Uses] appropriate speed/rate
[Initiates] conversation
[Attempts to] join a conversation
[Attempts to] maintain conversation
[Listens to] others
[Talks about] same subject
[Adjust to] others' mood/level of interest
[Changes subject] appropriately
[Shows growing awareness of] conversation breaking down
[Attempts to] repair conversation
[Shows growing awareness of] colloquial meanings common sayings simple social inferencing embedded meanings

Receptive language

Listening and remembering
[Can remember] objects/pictures shown then hidden
(2 3 4 5 6 7 8)
[Can repeat back] [2 3 4 5 6 7 8] digits
words [2 3 4 5 6 7 8 9 10]
non-words (e.g. mav, wem, lif, col, bux, etc.)
[Can repeat back in reverse order] [2 3 4 5 6 7 8] digits
Word finding
[Can recall] known vocabulary
[Can remember] a simple message within class a simple message within school to familiar adults to less familiar adults
[Can remember] a simple message from school to home with aide-memoire without aide-memoire
Listening
[Uses] good listening rules (good sitting, looking, waiting, turn-taking) in directed one-to-one activity/in directed group activity/in carpet time/story time
[Can correctly complete] sound lotto
[Can listen to and answer] simple questions straightforward directions
[Can join in] refrains in rhymes, stories, poems, songs
[Can follow] instructions one-word level (jump, stand up) two-word level (hold the handle, stop running, come here) three-word level (give it to me, line up by the door, Ben's table line up next please) 4-word level (put it on the table, red group put aprons on please, put curved shapes here)
[Can follow] longer instructions (for simple drawings, models, cooking . . .)
[Can follow] more complex instructions which include **before and after** instructions **during** a task which include **negatives**
[Can follow] instructions when has to **select** information (e.g. children with black hair jump 2 times) **Using /if/** (if you have black shoes stand up)
Using /except/ (everybody, except the Year 2s, go and line up)
Using /unless/ (line up unless you need to see me)
[Can listen and] play listening games such as Simon says
[Can follow] instructions in class inputs, PE, whole-school service . . .
[Can indicate] if has not understood [Can ask for help] if has not understood
[Can recognize and show understanding of] figures of speech similes metaphors
[Can make] simple predictions deductions

Social use of language
[Can engage in] pretend play
[Can use] imaginary items in play
[Can] parallel play
[Can] play co-operatively with others

[Uses] 'good sitting' 'good looking' 'good waiting'
'good turn-taking'
[Uses] appropriate volume when speaking
[Uses] appropriate speed when speaking
[Uses] appropriate expression/intonation (prosody) when speaking
[Can show understanding of] feelings/emotions (e.g. happy, sad, cross/angry, tired, energetic, worried, excited, afraid/frightened)
[Makes] appropriate eye contact
[Maintains] eye contact appropriately
[Greets] appropriately
[Recognizes] tones of voice
[Recognizes] facial expressions
[Recognizes] body language and commonly understood gestures
[Responds to] a range of expressions of feelings (e.g. happy, sad, cross/angry, tired, energetic, worried, excited, afraid/frightened)
[Uses] a range of expressions of feelings (e.g. happy, sad, cross/angry, tired, energetic, worried, excited, afraid/frightened)
[Responds appropriately to] social exchanges
[Responds appropriately to] teasing
[Uses] appropriate posture and distance in a range of conversational situations
[By sensible response/behaviour shows growing understanding of] the effect of direct personal comments
[By sensible response/behaviour shows growing understanding of] school rules
[By sensible response/behaviour shows growing understanding of] danger and safety
[Asks for] help appropriately
[Asserts] self appropriately

Developmental co-ordination difficulties and sensory integration

Pupils may initially be able, with great effort and concentration, **to produce one or two movements** such as hops or jumps. Later they will be able **to sustain** these movements and produce six, ten or more. Later still these movements will become **automatic**. These levels of skill need to be used in targets.

[Can] crawl
[Can] creep
[Can] stand well
[Can] walk steadily
[Can] walk on toes
[Can] walk on heels
[Can] walk heel to toe
[Can] walk along a bench
[Can] do up and down steps on alternate feet
[Can execute a] standing leg balance
[Can execute a] standing leg swing
[Can execute] standing circling toes

[Can execute a] good sitting to standing and vice versa
[Can execute a] squat balance
[Can] curled on back rock side to side
[Can] sit and spin
[Can] balance on knees
[Can execute] a bridge balance
[Can move] shoulders forwards and backwards singly and together
[Can execute a] standing scissor arm swing
[Can hold] a straight arm stretch
[Can] roll hop jump skip
[Can] throw, catch, bounce, dribble a ball
[Can] lying prone raise head, shoulders, chest with arms straight
[Can] lying on back raise each leg separately, then both legs together
[Can] move fingers apart and together several times
[Can] curl and stretch fingers
[Can] press each finger to thumb one at a time
[Can] with elbows at sides rotate each wrist in turn
[Can] pick up small objects (blocks, beads, paper clips)
[Can] build a nine-block tower
[Can] thread 5–10 small beads
[Can] wind laces round cotton reel
[Can] join 5–10 multi-link cubes
[Can] unscrew containers, jars, etc.
[Can] fasten zipper, buttons, buckles, laces
[Can] press and roll clay or similar to make spheres, snakes
[Can] hold a pencil to execute a 'frog's legs' movement
[Can] cut with scissors at age-appropriate level
[Can show a growing ability to] plan and organize
[Can show a growing ability to] track, shift gaze and interpret by looking
[Can show a growing ability to] tolerate and ignore visual distractions
[Can show a growing ability to] locate, identify and discriminate between sounds
[Can show a growing ability to] tolerate and ignore auditory distractions
[Can show a growing ability to] tolerate a range of tactile experiences (e.g. hair, nails being cut, tidying appearance, use of craft materials)
Is showing a growing awareness of and ability with vestibular sense (balance)
Is showing a growing awareness of and ability with proprioceptive sense (own body, position in space and how much force/pressure to use)

8

Behaviour

There is a growing body of research to suggest that there is a strong link between behavioural, emotional and social difficulties (BESD) and communication problems. **Pupils with SLI may also have BESD and pupils with BESD may also have SLI.**

Consider again the four areas of language development used in the targets above:

1 difficulties explaining, conveying information, making requests, stating needs – talking clearly (**Expressive language**);
2 difficulties understanding, remembering, learning and using even commonly understood vocabulary – understanding (**Receptive language**);
3 difficulties with understanding body language, facial expressions and gesture, in interpreting literally, with social language, with jokes, idioms, sarcasm, colloquialisms, in relating to others **(Social use of language – Pragmatics)**;
4 difficulties with self-organization, with judging movements and balance and with a range of sensory experiences – awkward and clumsy **(Developmental co-ordination and sensory integration)**.

It appears perfectly logical that children with SLI may have associated behaviour difficulties.

Possible action

- Assess pupils with BESD for SLI and vice versa.
- Use language targets for BESD pupils and behaviour targets for SLI pupils.
- Alert parents and all staff to the co-morbidity of SLI and BESD and offer awareness training. This can then lead to a change of attitude, modification of communicative style and of approach that in turn can support changes in the language understanding and language use of the pupil and consequent improvements in behaviour.

Behaviour targets

- The underlying language difficulties need to be addressed using targets given above.
- Acceptable behaviour in a range of situations and contexts needs to be broken down; ensure the language within instructions for acceptable behaviour is clearly understood, modelled and explained.
- It is helpful if a reference of such acceptable behaviours, using an adapted Carol Gray Social Story model, is readily accessible. (Use a personal memory file for a pupil or incorporate these in class systems by having them on a wall display or class book.)
- Liaison with parents/carers is essential so that there is consistency of language and expected behaviour in home and school.

Sample IEP – present level of performance

Name: Tilly Jones   Year: Reception   Date of Birth: 30.10.200X   CoP Stage: SA

School: Sunshine CPS   Class: 2   Teacher: Mrs Green

Has speech and language impairment and has particular difficulties with [highlight appropriately]:

Expressive language	Receptive language	Social use of language
• difficulty with clear, intelligible speech • difficulty with grammatical speech • difficulty with logical flowing speech • difficulty learning vocabulary	• difficulty following instructions • memory difficulties behaviours, codes • difficulty understanding language	• difficulty relating to others • difficulty with social behaviours, codes • difficulty with fast-paced playground games • literal understanding and use of language

Sensory integration difficulties	Developmental co-ordination difficulties (DCD)	Behaviour
• visual problems with tracking, shifting gaze and interpreting by looking • hearing problems with locating sounds, identifying and discriminating between sounds • problems with taste and smell – over- or under-reaction to particular tastes and smells, leading to restricted diet and dislike of 'hands-on' activities • tactile problems – over- or under-reaction to touch, dislike of hair or nails being cut, lack of awareness of nose running or food spilled on clothes, fiddling with everything • vestibular and proprioceptive difficulties with balance and body awareness	• difficulties with whole body movements and balance • difficulties with manipulative skills • difficulties with organization and planning	• unacceptable behaviours • difficulty with focused attention, listening

Present level of performance of Expressive language, Receptive language, Social use of language, Sensory and co-ordination skills and behaviour.
(Teacher assessment or appropriate test scores)

Tilly seems to have significant speech production difficulties. She may have a fluctuating hearing loss. She has memory and recall difficulties, sequencing difficulties. All the above are significantly impacting on her learning and socializing.

17 March referred for a speech and language therapy assessment and to Audiology for a hearing assessment.

8

Sample IEP current targets

Name: Tilly Jones Year: Reception Date of Birth: 30.10.200X CoP Stage: SA
School: Sunshine CPS Class: 2 Teacher: Mrs Green

Date	Target	Outside agencies involved	School staff involved	Resources	Date to be assessed	Progress made
24 March	Given lots of encouragement will attempt to answer register		Class teacher and NNEB	Good talking reward stickers	10 May	
24 March	Given lots of encouragement and in a group will join in and attempt to produce loud and quiet sounds with voice in music sessions		Class teacher – using percussion instruments to make loud and quiet sounds then voices – shout and whisper a range of sounds such as /ah/ee/oh/etc.	Good talking reward stickers	10 May	
24 March	Can produce one-word labels for food vocabulary (food chosen as it is part of class topic work)		1:1 short daily sessions with NNEB playing games with food vocabulary cards. Mum to use this vocabulary when shopping, Tilly to help	A quiet space to work in Food reward stickers	10 May	
24 March	Can jump taking 2 feet off the ground and maintain balance		Short daily exercise session with two friends and NNEB	Space in hall or outside		

Date of review meeting 10 May or earlier if speech therapy or Audiology have been in touch.

Those to be invited

Signed Parent . . . . SENCo . . . . Class teacher . . . .

8

Sample IEP – outcome of review

Name: Tilly Jones | Year: Reception | Date of Birth: 30.10.200X | CoP Stage: SA

School: Sunshine CPS | Class: 2 | Teacher: Mrs Green

Outcome of review

School comments

Tilly's Audiology appointment has been arranged in three weeks time and she has a speech and language therapy appointment in two weeks; school will write a short report for Mum to take to the appointments.

- She will answer the register now with encouragement. We will continue to encourage and praise this.
- She is beginning to join in at music time with loud and quiet sound making. This will continue and some tapping of rhythms of class names and known, topic vocabulary will be added.
- She has done well with learning and recalling food vocabulary; this will now be consolidated by being used in some games that encourage the use of more than a one-word label/using sentence patterns such as 'This is a . . .', 'I like/I don't like', 'I eat ______ for breakfast/dinner/tea'.
- Tilly can jump 2 to 3 times but jumping is not yet automatic so this will continue daily. Some balance exercises and cross lateral exercises will be added.

Parents' comments

We are pleased that Tilly is getting this help; we will try to help her at home with the games and with jumping.

Pupil's comments

Tilly came into the review meeting at the end to see everyone. We said how pleased everyone was with her hard work and that she was answering the register and learning some new words. When asked if she liked playing the word games and doing the exercises she smiled and nodded.

Outcome of review

School will hope to liaise with Audiology and speech and language therapy when the assessments have been completed. New targets as outlined above will be set and another review will take place in six weeks.

8

9 Parents as Part of the Team

9

Reviews of the literature and personal experience have provided convincing evidence of the effectiveness of parental involvement in promoting children's education

Hornby, G., *Working with Parents of Children with Special Needs* (1995) Cassell

Developing effective parent–professional working is beneficial for all those involved. But like everything else it requires careful thought and planning. To establish effective parent–professional partnerships it is necessary:

- to establish a climate wherein contributions from either party are valued and respected;
- for professionals to increase their knowledge and understanding of the parent perspective and check that parents have a clear idea of the school's expectations;
- to develop good communication and counselling skills.

The three quotes below illustrate the experiences of some parents of children with speech and language impairment and highlight some points for consideration.

'There were times when I collapsed with a thumping head or just sat and cried because there seemed no way out – no one knew what to do for J, where to send him, it seemed hopeless.'

'We carry on trying to do all the ordinary things you know but he doesn't understand much really. Then one day when you're not expecting it he gets it, he really understands and it's just great, more than great really. It takes him twice, three times as long as other children but that makes it so great when he gets there.'

'She has made us so proud ... she has had an excellent report and has been chosen to be presented with an achievement award for maths.
We were so worried when we found out about her speech and language disorder. We weren't very hopeful of her achieving at school but her determination, hard work and all the help she has received is paying off.
I hope that if any ... parents have the same fears and worries I had, they will feel encouraged by what M has achieved and hopefully what she will continue to achieve. There is light at the end of the tunnel.'

Parents may have a frustrating time trying to get their child's difficulties recognized and then a struggle trying to secure an appropriate placement or appropriate support. Be aware when first meeting parents of children with speech and language difficulties that the stressful time they have had may affect the way they approach you.

9

- Plan for a smooth and happy start in school to reassure pupil and parents.
- Establish a good system of communication with parents. Even if the school already has a system in place, consider whether it meets the needs of parents of pupils with special needs, including those with speech and language impairment. Such parents will benefit from more frequent meetings and exchanges of information. It is beneficial for parents and professionals to work together on any individual targets and regular liaison is needed for this too. Some schools use a daily diary system, others use the reading diary that goes home regularly, while still others prefer to talk at the end of each day. Whatever system is chosen it needs to be one that suits both school and parents.
- Consider a system for emergencies. Some children with speech and language impairment will not show any anxiety or unhappiness at school but will wait until they get home. Parents are then left in a frustrating and unhappy position, with a distraught child who may not sleep that night and will probably refuse to go to school the next day.
- Consider potentially difficult times – both inside and outside the classroom situation (speech therapy, special needs sessions, transition from one key stage to another, from mainstream to specialist provision or from specialist provision to mainstream).
- Raise awareness, among all staff and volunteer helpers, of speech and language difficulties and effective ways of helping children.
- Be aware of the strain that parents may be under. Living with a child with language difficulties can prove exhausting.
- Continue to be sensitive as to how any messages or information about progress, or lack of it, may be received. Parents may experience a wide range of emotions, from anger through despair to hope.
- Having considered how best to support pupils with speech and language impairment in your educational setting, try to implement strategies as whole-class or whole-school strategies. Whole-school listening and playground strategies can benefit not just the children with speech and language impairment, but all children in school.
- Be very clear to parents about whole-school and whole-class strategies and support, as well as any individual support their child will be receiving.
- Find out about local and national support agencies and information centres, and help parents to decipher the educational jargon in official documents.

For parents of children with special needs there is often no clear path, expectations and assumptions have to be constantly revised, there is shock, bewilderment, isolation and sadness and anger and at the same time there is often pressure (self-imposed or from outside) to take action, to make decisions and to 'deal with' the situation.

Blamires, M. *et al.*, *Parent Teacher Partnership* (1997) *David Fulton*

Reviews

Whether through a review of the child's statement of special educational need, or the school's own monitoring system, more formal meetings will need to take place at least once a year. These

For parents almost any meeting about their child feels like a crisis meeting.
Blamires, M. *et al.* (1997)

meetings need careful planning so that they can be as relaxed, informative and useful as possible.

- Give enough time and information in advance so that each person attending can contribute. Consider giving a brief framework of the areas to be discussed so questions and points can be thought through, jotted down and brought to the meeting. Parents may welcome some help in compiling their own contribution. If this is established procedure for parents and professionals then such points can be discussed in a non-threatening way.
- Offer parents the opportunity to bring a friend so they don't feel quite so outnumbered by professionals.
- Consider the environment in which the meeting will be held. It needs to be a place where the meeting can proceed without interruption. The furniture needs to be arranged so the room is welcoming and relaxed.
- Appoint a facilitator and a scribe. The facilitator should invite each person present to speak and ensure there is time for everyone to make a contribution. The facilitator should also feed back regularly throughout the meeting what has been discussed and decided, and at the close of the meeting summarize the main points and decisions. The scribe should keep an eye on the time and be responsible for taking minutes that will be distributed to all those present as soon as possible after the meeting.
- All those present need to be introduced or to introduce themselves.
- Check your body language to ensure it is welcoming and attentive.
- Guard against giving an honest but totally negative report.
- Engage in active listening – show that you really want to hear what others have to say, respect their feelings and opinions even if they differ from your own.
- Try not to take expressions of strong feelings, rage or sadness personally.
- Deal with any friction or distress sensitively; ask questions to elicit more information, e.g. 'Can you tell us why this is annoying/upsetting you?'
- Allow everyone to make final comments and set a date for the next meeting.

'I'll tell you what it's like sometimes. He doesn't understand and stamps and screams in a rage. His grandparents and my sister criticize me for not disciplining him, they don't understand and think I should be firm with him. He's upset, I'm upset and in the middle his brother wants help with his homework. It's exhausting.'

These may seem to be very basic points but I have found that a checklist based on these points ensures meetings are friendly and useful.

Working together

Be ready to work with parents but be wary of overburdening them. Sarah Newman (*Small Steps Forward*, Jessica Kingsley) (1999) wrote:

All the specialists bombard you with leaflets and things to do and you feel you should be doing everything all at once or that you are never doing enough and sometimes your child is unresponsive or unco-operative and you feel overwhelmed and an abject failure.

Accept that, for some parents, just surviving the ordinary daily routine is all they can manage, while for others just doing ordinary family things is worthwhile and more than enough. Such parents may not be able to become so involved for a variety of reasons, ranging from lack of confidence to work commitments. They may need more direct support and it may require more time and effort to establish and maintain good communication. Many parents may still be coming to terms with their child's impairment and will need sensitivity and understanding. (Garry Hornby compares this to the grieving process. His thoughts on this are very helpful in gaining some understanding of the feelings of parents of children with special needs.)

Other parents will be, or will become, very knowledgeable about speech and language impairment and will wish to be very involved in supporting their child. They will be active members of the team, probably coming into school to work alongside staff, if this is your policy. When this type of arrangement is established it can be beneficial for all, especially the child concerned.

Children with speech and language difficulties need opportunities to practise their developing speech and language skills. They need opportunities to experience a range of language concepts and vocabulary at first hand. They may need to improve their co-ordination skills. Parents and other family members can help with all of these. In fact, by providing opportunities in their home environments they are providing different contexts and helping their child both to generalize and to consolidate learning. Some things are done better at home – there are banks of vocabulary that are much more meaningful when experienced outside school – animals, vehicles, etc. It is easier to have extended conversations at home and to have the undivided attention of a person or small group of people.

Parents and professionals working together can help their children learn in a more complete and holistic way, and often at a faster pace. Certainly, and perhaps most importantly of all, when partnership working is successful and a child makes progress, the sense of achievement and joy is felt by all those involved – pupil, parent and professional.

'I was at the end of my tether when T eventually got some support, exhausted and drained. I wanted him to get help but I wanted him to not need it, to be in an ordinary class. So I was down too, a bit depressed. I thought it was all my fault. Then things began to change.

The first thing was he was happier, he loved going to school. And then I started to come in and watch you, what you did, and I'd tell you what he'd done at home and you'd tell me about school, good and bad so we could work together. It was easier, I didn't get so fraught because we helped each other. Now he's making progress with some things but not much with others, like maths. But he's getting the help he needs and we've started to feel hopeful about the future.'

10 How Can You Help Your Child?

Children learn faster and better when their parents are involved.

There is a great deal that parents, carers and other family members can do to help a child with speech and language difficulties. You will help your child by just 'being there' for him; listening to him, talking to him, showing him that you are interested in what he says and does and proud of his achievements, no matter how small they are.

The single most important requirement in terms of development is your child's self-confidence. Help him to believe in himself and have the confidence to try.

Avoid talking to other adults about your child's difficulties in front of him – it will only reinforce his feeling that he is a 'problem'. Help his brothers and sisters, grandma and grandad to understand how to help as well. There are some ideas below – you will think of many more yourself, because you know your child better than anyone else.

The home is the ideal place to provide a wide range of experiences in a secure and loving setting.

At mealtimes ask your child to put the peelings in the bin, or to lay the table. You could talk about:

- **Utensils** – cutlery, pots, pans, etc., what they are called, what they are made of, what they are used for.
- **Food** – where it was grown, how it got to the shop, what sort of shop, how it was prepared, how it was cooked, its colour, its shape, its texture, its taste.
- **Positions** – who is sitting next to whom, opposite whom, at the top of the table, on the left or the right.
- **Time** – what time it is when you eat, morning, afternoon, evening, late, early, what you did first, second, etc., what you did before the meal and what you will do after the meal, what you always do at mealtimes and what you never do.

It should be an enjoyable time so make a game out of it. Perhaps take it in turns to say one thing about an object or play 'I spy something made of metal', or sing the names of the food to a tune you both know. Choose one thing at a time rather than trying to do everything at once.

Rhymes, songs and stories are beneficial for many reasons: rhythm, listening, remembering, labelling, answering questions, vocabulary, eye contact, turn-taking and having fun. You can enjoy these in the bath, at bedtime, waiting for the bus or driving along in the car.

Homemade scrapbooks and photograph albums with photographs of the child himself and other family members are great for learning vocabulary and extending language. He can add drawings, labels and tickets from trips out, programmes from the pantomime, etc.

General guidance

Reward your child for his efforts. Whatever the quality of your child's speech and language, reward a good try, pay attention, smile, touch, praise and repeat back what has been said. Of course if you know your child can do a little better with some positive encouragement then give some but do make allowances for tiredness, lack of confidence and bad days. If your child has difficulty talking, give him time and encouragement.

Speak clearly. It is important that your child hears you using good, clear language. Your own speech can be simplified and used alongside gesture to gear down to the child's level of understanding. When the child makes a mistake, try one of these approaches rather than simply correcting him.

Restating: child – 'dog'
adult – 'yes, look the **horse** is running.'
Gently point out the correct word then find opportunities to use it a lot.
Expanding: child – 'car, car'
adult – 'yes, it's a police car and it's going fast.'
Prompting: adult – 'it's not a dog it's a …'
child – 'horse'
adult – 'well remembered, the horse is …,'
Recasting: child – 'horse likes grass'
adult – 'yes, the horse is eating grass. <pause> Grass is good food for horses.'

In this way you have repeated back what the child has said, making him feel good, but you've changed it just enough to reinforce a word you're practising (horse) and you've introduced some new language (food).

If your child is passive and rarely starts talking or rarely responds, try:

- responding enthusiastically to any reaction from him, whether it's a sound or a gesture or just a glance at you;
- repeating the sound or gesture and telling him it is good that he is joining in;
- using favourite routines and nursery rhymes until he responds in some way.

The less a child talks the more opportunities and encouragement are needed.

If your child stutters there are some ways you can help. Don't focus on the stuttering or label your child as a stutterer. Don't ask him to slow down or try to think about what he is saying. Try not to finish sentences for him. Do give him the same chances to talk as everyone else in the family and give him time. Make sure he has his turn in family talk and doesn't have to fight to be heard. Listen to what he says and answer or comment on that, not on how he says it. Notice which situations seem to worry your child and be ready to help him.

This could be when visitors come or when he is questioned directly, for instance.

If your child has difficulty understanding you can help by making sure he is looking at you and you have his full attention. Use words your child knows. Use short, simple sentences. Try and talk about what is happening or has only just happened. Try to make talking good fun and so increase your child's confidence.

Try to choose good times to practise when neither you nor your child is too tired. Remember, if given a few pointers, other family members will probably be keen to help. Grandparents or older brothers and sisters can provide different ways of practising while having fun. 'Little and often' is a good rule of thumb.

Avoid outbursts of frustration by finding ways for your child to release pent-up energy in activity such as football, swimming, catch, walking, bike riding, gardening, dusting or polishing. Many parents find the time just after their child gets home from school difficult. Talk with the teacher and plan some activities with your child, to establish a routine for arriving home.

Good manners: parents and other family members can also help specifically with the demonstration of acceptable social codes and behaviour such as taking turns and saying 'please' and 'thank you'.

You can help your child develop his memory by sending him to fetch things and by giving him messages to take to other family members in and around the house. If he needs a lot of help with this at first, give very short messages and if necessary draw a little picture for him to carry in case he forgets, or write the words down if he can read them. You can very gradually lengthen the messages or the distance or time over which he will try to remember.

Friends are important. Help your child to make and develop friendships. School can be a lonely place without friends and the world outside school even lonelier. It may mean extra effort in overseeing friendships by inviting friends round, arranging outings to the park, etc. and supervising these more closely than for other children. Rainbows, Beavers, Brownies, Cubs, dance classes, gym classes and swimming classes have all proved helpful and enjoyable for some children. It is sometimes advisable to have a private word with the group organizer first to explain the kinds of difficulties your child might have. They are usually most understanding.

Many children with speech and language difficulties find friendships difficult and are vulnerable because of this. They can become targets for bullying. One way to deal with this is to build up a good group of friends who will support and look after each other.

10

What's wrong with him?

It can be difficult to know what to say when friends and neighbours ask what's wrong with your child. Do think it through before someone asks, though, and choose a way of explaining that is comfortable for you. Here are some suggestions that have worked for other parents:

- My son is bright and able but he has a particular difficulty with language.
- She needs help to learn to speak clearly.
- He needs help to understand language.
- If you're not understanding her don't worry, I don't sometimes. Try asking her to show you or just leave it and perhaps say, 'I know you are working hard to talk more clearly and I will be able to understand you better soon if you keep on working hard'
- If you think he is not understanding don't worry, try saying it again more simply by 'chunking' what you're saying into shorter sentences with pauses in between.
- Please carry on talking with her because she enjoys talking with you and it helps her.

Some suggestions for games

- **Kim's game:** Prepare a tray of five or six small items. Give the child a chance to look at them then cover the tray and remove one item. Ask, 'What is missing?' You can gradually increase the number of items that are removed and that have to be remembered. Or use a magazine picture with a number of items. Let the child look at it then cover it and get him to try to remember as many items as he can.

- Arrange two or three items in order. Have the child close his eyes while you mix them up. Can he put them back in order? You can do the same with a few coloured crayons or blocks.

- Write three numbers or letters then cover them up. Can he write them on his paper?
- Cut up the simple comic strip stories from a child's comic and have him put them in order and tell the story.
- Complete jigsaws making sure you guide your child to look for pieces that fit together because of their shape, colour or what item or part item is on them. If your child finds jigsaws difficult, give him an almost-completed puzzle, with two or three pieces missing, and let him try to complete it. Gradually increase the number of missing pieces.
- Help to develop memory by playing games where your child has to listen and then do several actions. Example: Hop to the door, touch the floor, turn around twice and sit down.
- Give your child three or four items in a pile then call out an order. When you've finished speaking he has to put the items in that order. Let him have a turn at telling you as well. You can do this with numbers, letters and words.
- I went to the shop and I bought ... Usually in this game players choose an item in turn, following the letters of the alphabet (apple, banana, carrot, date, egg ...) You could adapt it by giving different categories, e.g. food, shapes, animals, tools, and play as above or have a maximum number of items to be remembered.
  First player: I went to the shops and I bought a sandwich.
  Second player: I went to the shops and I bought a sandwich and a bag of crisps.
  Third player: I went to the shops and I bought a sandwich, a bag of crisps and some biscuits ...
- Rhymes: use currently popular songs or nursery rhymes. Sing or say them, leaving a pause for your child to give the rhyming word (Baa, baa, black sheep, have you any wool? Yes sir, yes sir, three bags ____.) (Uh-oh, I'm in trouble, someone's come along and hey burst my____.), etc. Or make up your own, like this – I'm thinking of something that rhymes with bun. It shines in the sky. It is the ____.
- I Spy: play the original by all means (I spy something beginning with ...) but it can also be adapted for almost any language work. 'I spy something rough/smooth, big/small, a vehicle, something that's red ...'
- Read a short story and after your child has listened to it, he can tell it to you or draw pictures in order. This can also be done with well-known or favourite stories.

Old favourites: don't forget all the usual activities and games that are valuable and fun:

- Read to your child. Sit side by side sometimes so that your child can see the text and see your finger moving along under the print. Ask what might happen next or, with a longer story, recap the story so far each time you read a chapter.
- Watch television together. There are some really interesting

programmes these days and some parents have found a selection of videos on colour, animals, vehicles, etc. really helpful. Then you will have a shared context to talk about.

- Hunt the Thimble, Snakes and Ladders and Ludo are all good for practising position words and the Hokey Cokey is great for left and right. Snap and Dominoes help develop careful looking.
- Puzzles books and comics may have dot to dot, mazes and colouring; fun ways to practise pencil control. Comics and puzzle books also have pictures to talk about and spot the difference games that are excellent for language work and fun to do.
- Some children need to practise balancing, running, jumping and other movement skills. Bike riding and ball games are outdoor fun and skills that some of our children need to practise a lot. Swimming is an excellent and fun activity. Some children have been greatly helped by going to a gym club.

Older children

As children grow up and strive to become more independent, it is important to help them help themselves. Some simple equipment can be a big help:

- A smart Filofax in which to jot things down that may otherwise be forgotten, such as party invitations, trips, etc. It can also contain vital information such as personal addresses, phone numbers, dates of birth and emergency plans for who to phone and where to go when things go wrong.
- A very small cassette recorder if jotting things down is difficult because of writing and handwriting problems.
- A clear pencil case so the contents are visible. Two sets of pens, ruler, etc., one for homework, one for school.
- A talking watch, available from the RNIB, PO Box 173, Peterborough, PE2 6WS.

Discuss with your child how in some situations some people will not understand them and maybe your child will not understand what they mean either. Discuss possible strategies;

- 'I'm not very good with words.'
  'I don't understand.'
  'Could you write it down please.'
  'Can you tell me another way please.'
  'I'll just leave it for now thank you.'
- Phone home for help. Teach them to always check that they have coins for the phone and/or a phone card. As a back-up, teach them how to make a reverse charge call.
- Sometimes in peer group situations it may be best to walk away.

When giving instructions say them more than once, then have your child repeat them back to you. If there is quite a lot of information to remember try to make it as simple as possible.

- Encourage your child to repeat the instruction silently to himself while on the way to do it.
- Try using visual imagery (pictures in the mind) to help the memory. If your child is sent to buy milk, bread and a newspaper, make it clear there are three things to remember, then make a funny picture like reading the paper with a glass of milk in one hand and a sandwich in the other.
- Try using pictures, maps and diagrams as well.
- Sticky note pads are excellent for this as they can be stuck up for a time, then easily removed when not needed.
- Most importantly, have the children make up or choose their own ways of remembering and have them write their own reminder notes and lists. In this way they will become more self-reliant.

School survival

Children need to consider what difficulties they are having and how they can use their strengths to help themselves in different contexts: general organization, working in class, breaktimes, homework and exams.

- Instead of parents remembering and packing games kit, swimming kit, etc. children should learn to do so themselves. Have a weekly timetable in a conspicuous place and check it at a regular time every day.
- It is useful to carry a basic toolkit that includes pens, calculator, inhaler, etc., and it should be the child's responsibility to organize replacements.
- In class, children need to think about sitting in a good place in the room to help them with their work. This might mean away from the distractions of the window or near to the middle where they can hear and see well. They need to make sure there is enough space on the table or desk to get out what is needed. Then settle down to listen and remember to look at the teacher when she is speaking.
- Discuss a range of strategies for breaks and lunchtimes. What are the rules and procedures for these times? Discuss strategies for joining a group, leaving a group and possible responses to current peer-group jargon. What is the dinner menu? Discuss possible choices.
- Bullying can sometimes occur, for a variety of reasons. Some children are not good at fast peer-group talk, which can change rapidly as new words and phrases come into fashion. They may have difficulty following the rules of current games and may not understand jokes. This makes them vulnerable. One of the best ways round this is to have a good friend or friends. Although you

cannot force particular children to be your child's friend, you can help by being involved in their social life. You can encourage and support through being a willing taxi, giving invitations home to tea and invitations to come on trips, and by being aware which after-school clubs or groups it might be helpful for your child to join.

- Homework is something else that needs organizing. Your child will benefit from you taking an interest in his homework and, sometimes, helping him with it. Even if you don't know a lot about science or history, just helping him to understand the task and plan out his work will be of benefit. Most schools have a homework jotter in which the homework task is listed, with the handing-in date. It is essential for children to use this conscientiously.
- It is helpful to have homework partners or at least have the phone numbers of one or two reliable friends who are doing the same homework.
- It may be possible to put some homework on to tape rather than writing all assignments, or for your child to dictate for you to write. Such possibilities need to be discussed with the school.
- Children should not be spending long hours on homework every night and if this becomes the case then the situation needs to be discussed with the school.

Make sure you have the name and number of a member of staff who is your contact person at the school. Then, if you have any queries or something goes wrong you have an immediate contact.

Parental faith and support are probably the most important things that any parent can give their child. So, apart from the practical ideas given above, try and keep a positive attitude. That and a sense of humour will see you through.

11 Concluding Thoughts

Children with speech and language impairment may present with a range of difficulties affecting all areas of the curriculum and they may be viewed as having significant special educational needs.

Conversely, if approached another way, all curriculum areas can be used to support the development of language skills and learning in general by acknowledging that some children learn differently. Then it is a short step to planning for this different learning:

- **Speech production** – Clear, flowing speech, conversation skills and question and answer techniques can be practised as part of group and class discussions within a supportive environment wherein any contribution is welcomed and praised and 'good thinking' is highlighted, demonstrated and discussed.
- **Vocabulary** – Vocabulary can be prioritized within each curriculum subject, flagged up at the start of the session, briefly recapped during and at the end of a session, and used during follow-up work.
- **Grammar** – Grammar is an important part of literacy work but can also be part of developing recording skills in other curriculum areas, directly taught.
- **Listening skills** – A whole-school approach works best: short introductory inputs, reminders and praise for specific listening behaviours (good sitting, good looking, good thinking, turn-taking).
- **Understanding** – Check understanding regularly in a variety of different ways, throughout every lesson.
- **Memory skills** – These are part of listening and understanding as pupils are called upon to remember the vocabulary and knowledge content of a session. Short revision times can be built into any lesson, with pupils using supportive aids if appropriate.
- **Social use of language techniques** – These are part of good listening and part of a whole-school behaviour and discipline policy. In addition they can be addressed during PSHE and RE sessions.
- **Acceptable behaviour** – This too is part of a whole-school behaviour and discipline policy. Teaching acceptable behaviours can be carried out in context during the school day – e.g. quieter voices in class/louder in PE, or how to organize sharing equipment, acceptable ways forward, who to go to and how to ask for help when a task seems impossible.
- **Co-ordination** – Specific extra daily sessions to develop motor skills are relatively easy to build into the school day. Short warm-up sessions for whole-body movement or manipulative skills can be built in at lining-up times as well as at the beginning of lessons – PE or writing, art, design or cookery.

- **Sensory integration** – Short tasks or routines to develop sensory integration can be built into daily class routines – such as a feelings board, movement breaks, posture cushions and legitimate 'fiddle toys' alongside the use of multi-sensory techniques.

In our busy, over-full school days anything that takes extra time at the planning stage may initially seem to be unhelpful. However, the population of children with speech and language difficulties is significant, and some of these children will remain in mainstream classes for most, if not all, of their education. There is a need then for colleagues, in both specialist and mainstream settings, to increase their knowledge of speech and language difficulties and how best to support these children. It would be helpful if many of the suggestions that have been given become part of general good practice so that all children, those with particular special needs and those without, will benefit. All pupils benefit from clear and straightforward instructional language and from clear target setting based on individual needs. So in the long term time is saved, as teaching becomes more effective for all pupils.

Speech and language impairment is a relatively new field of study and as such we are learning more about it all the time. The ideas given in this book are offered in a spirit of collaborative working and it is hoped that, as practitioners in the classroom situation, colleagues in mainstream will work with specialist teachers to improve on current practice and make school an enjoyable and successful experience for all children.

Mrs M: *Why do we come to school?*

C: *I know, I know it's . . . we learn . . . we learn . . . we learn* ***everything****.*

Mrs M: *OK, and why do you think it's important to learn at school?*

C: *Good thinking, we learn good thinking . . . cos when we are growned ups . . . it will . . . it will be a good earth and we can have a* ***good time****.*

Appendix 1 Stages of Language Development

The developmental stages outlined below have been taken from a number of sources, including Sheridan *et al.* and Crystal. They can only ever be a very rough guide, and care should be taken, particularly when working with parents, to ensure an understanding of the wide variation in patterns of 'normal' development.

Expressive language

1–9 months

- **1 month** – startled by loud noises, stiffens, blinks and may cry. At first all cries are pure reflex but by six weeks there are different cries for hunger, discomfort, etc. This is the beginning of communication. There may be reflex babbling.
- By **3 months** – there is a definite response to mother's voice, vocalization when spoken to, may turn towards sound.
- By **6 months** – turns immediately to mother's voice across a room, vocalizes tunefully with single and double sounds, lots of babbling, intonation patterns emerging and often recognizable.

9–18 months

- **9-12 months** – vocalizes deliberately, shouts to attract attention, listens and shouts again. Babbles tunefully, echoes sounds and simplified words with no understanding, some imitation of adult sounds. Responds to own name and understands 'no' and 'bye bye' and accompanying gestures.
- By **12 months** – shows understanding of several words in context, recognizes his/her own name and familiar names such as 'dinner', 'car', etc. Uses Dada, Mama and a few other common nouns. Comprehends simple commands given with gestures – 'Give it to Daddy', 'Clap hands'. Uses one or two words with understanding.
- By **15 months** – spoken vocabulary of between 6-10 words, mostly nouns, verbs and other words such as 'more', 'there', 'all', 'gone', 'yes', 'no', familiar names and some question words such as 'what', 'where', 'who'. Jabbers loudly and freely, using a wide range of inflection and phonetic units, experiments with sounds. Vocalizes wishes and needs, points to familiar persons, animals or toys when requested. Understands many more than 6–10 words and obeys simple commands such as 'Shut the door', 'Give me the ball'.

18 months–2 years

- A spoken vocabulary of 6–20 words and understands many more. Uses jargon and much gesture. Often echoes last word of what is said to him. Demands desired objects by pointing and loud, urgent vocalization of single words. Tries to sing, enjoys nursery rhymes and tries to join in.
- By **2 years** – more verbal expression, less jargon. Uses 50 or more words and understands many more. May begin to join words to make simple sentences. A vocabulary of around 50 words is needed before two words are meaningfully combined, e.g. 'car go', 'it hot'. Word order is not yet fixed so utterances such as 'bark doggie', 'mummy where?' could be produced. Questions using question words and rising intonation are asked, such as 'who there?', 'Daddy gone?'. Negatives are formed by using 'no' or 'not' before nouns and verbs, such as 'not run', 'no more'. The prepositions 'in', 'on', the word ending '-ing' as in 'boy running' are emerging. Plural 's' as in 'shoes' or 'cats' is emerging. Past tense marker '-ed' as in 'baby falled' is emerging.

2–2½ years

A vocabulary of around 250 words. The beginnings of concept formation: toys, pictures and language begin to represent real objects in the child's mind. Ideas and information start to be expressed in language.

- Three element sentences such as 'Daddy kick ball', 'where go now', 'me want biccy', 'the red car' are now produced.
- Pronouns (I, me, you, he, she, that, this, mine, yours) begin to be used.
- Copula verb ('to be') is used as in 'I am cross', 'he is baby', 'you are big', 'cat be hurt'.
- Auxiliary verbs (have, do, may, can) with a main verb start to be used as in 'I can do', 'she is looking', 'me do like'.
- Between 2 and 3½ years the following word endings emerge: Past participle – I have seen/walked/talked/gone/taken/had. Third person singular 's' – he/she/it/says, walks, etc. Possessive – Mummy's bag, John's dog. Contracted negative – I won't/can't/don't. Contracted copula – I'm hot, he's good, Daddy's here. Contracted auxiliary – I've got three, he's going home. Superlative – fattest, biggest, happiest. Comparative – bigger, prettier, nicer. Adverb '-ly' – quickly, slowly, softly.

2½ years–3 years

Significant increase in vocabulary, now able to generalize, uses complex sentences and develops extended imaginary symbolic play sequences. Carries on simple conversations and is able to verbalize past experiences. Asks lots of questions, though many are meaningless. Words may still be simplified and telescoped. Listens to and enjoys stories, very attached to certain ones, which are demanded over and over again.

- Sentences of four and more elements are used, such as 'Susie going to town today'. Adjectives are joined together in a sentence as in 'A big red ball'.
- Nouns and adjectives are joined by 'and' - 'boys and girls', 'wet and muddy'.
- Two auxiliary verbs may be used together - 'he will be going'.
- Uses plurals and pronouns.

3–3½ years

Vocabulary continues to develop. Sentence length increases.

- Multiple sentences of more than one clause, i.e. containing more than one verb, are now produced. Simple statements are joined by conjunctions (and, when, because) - 'he sang and the girl danced', 'he'll come when I shout', 'he's tired because it's late'.
- Relative and nominal clauses such as 'the lady who saw me', 'the box that they put it in' and clauses used as objects of the verb, as in 'I don't want you to read that book'.
- Prepositions begin to appear.
- Comparative phrases such as 'he is bigger than you' begin to be used.

3½–4½ years

Speech completely intelligible, showing only a few infantile substitutions. Gives correct account of recent events and experiences, gives address and age. Asks lots of meaningful questions. Less egocentric in language, listens to and tells longer stories, confusing fact and fiction at times. Understands prepositions. Starts to know colours accurately.

- The use of auxiliary verbs is extended to include 'ought', 'might', 'should', 'must'.
- The use of passive structures begins to emerge, such as 'it's getting painted', 'the boy was bitten'.
- 'All', 'much', 'both', 'many' appear at the beginning of a noun phrase - 'all the people', 'both my sisters'.
- Pronoun errors such as 'her doing it' still occur.

4½+ years

- The different types of comparative, such as 'prettier' versus 'more beautiful', are learned.
- Sentence connecting devices and comment clauses such as 'actually', 'you know', and fillers such as 'sort of' begin to be used.

- The child may not fully understand: passive sentences, subordinating conjunctions (although, unless, since), verbs such as 'promise', 'ask', 'tell', adjectives such as 'eager to', 'easy to', 'hard to' and 'anxious to'.

5 years

A vocabulary of around 1,500–2,000 words. Prepositions used appropriately and to give directions. 'Why' questions asked and responses listened to. Speech generally more fluent and accurate; however, confusion with fricatives (s, f, th) often still remains. Refers to concrete nouns by use and asks the meaning of abstract words. Language is much more purposeful. Loves stories and will act them out, live them.

6 years

A vocabulary of around 3,000 words, with good articulation. Use of verb tenses, past and future, emerging with a degree of accuracy (future concept is harder than that of the past). Beginning to be able to relate ideas and understand cause and effect. Interested in written language and able to relate own experiences to those in books.

Language development continues after the age of 6 in a number of important areas. Vocabulary and word-meaning expansion are the most obvious aspects of later language development but other high-level language skills are important:

- comprehending beyond the actual words in a text (inference);
- understanding a range of colloquial terms;
- understanding double and implied meanings;
- understanding puns, plays on words and jokes;
- more complex spelling and grammar skills.

Failure to expand language competence beyond the basic level reached at 6 can frequently pass unnoticed. There are important consequences, however, for intellectual development and for learning and performance in school.

The development of pragmatic skills – the use of language for social interaction

First few months of life – eye contact established between mother and child.

3 months – child's gaze follows adult's, leading to joint attention of other objects. Parents and carers respond to the child's noises as if they are intentional communication, which establishes an early basis for dialogue and later conversation.

3–6 months – turn-taking games such as 'peekaboo' develop – these are important for facilitating parent–child interaction, and adults start including nearby objects and actions in these to-and-fro language games. This relies heavily on shared attention and eye contact to associate words and things.

12+ months – as the child's language emerges, more vocalization than gesture is used. Conversation starts and from 1 year onwards children begin to consciously play with language, using silly voices for animals, etc.

2–3 years – children develop linguistic strategies in order to gain attention – they use focusing remarks to prepare someone else for action, e.g. Child: 'You see that train.' Adult: 'Yes.' Child:'Well, I want it.'

They also try out language games on parents. They make, and can respond to, simple requests, and can make statements or comments. They become increasingly aware of the social functions of communication and begin to learn to negotiate. At 2, this may simply mean pushing another child out of the way and grabbing the bike!

By **3 years** – children have generally acquired the ability to make and respond to clarification requests, and stylistic variations of language are heard in role-play (e.g. they use features of 'Daddy's' speech when pretending to be Daddy).

By **4 years** – children are beginning to 'read between the lines', i.e. to perceive the intention behind the speech. For example, they can understand reasoned responses, e.g. Child: 'Can I go out now?' Adult: 'It's raining. Why not play with the train?'

There is an increased capacity to joke and to lie. Children at this age can learn in a group of other children and can negotiate with others, using language to sort out problems and to build on prior learning.

By 4–6 years – children are able to hold quite complicated conversations. The following skills are appearing and continue to develop as the child grows up:

- They can see when a conversation is breaking down and request clarification or try to repair the conversation: 'Did you mean that one?' or 'What do you mean?'
- They can join and finish a conversation appropriately, using non-verbal and verbal strategies: making or breaking eye contact, saying 'Can I just say this?' or 'Thanks, bye'.
- They can assess and use knowledge of different social contexts and personal characteristics and use appropriate body language, gesture, tone of voice and expression. They can adjust to others' moods and levels of interest.
- They can refer back to the past and forward to the future and use world knowledge, showing understanding of colloquialisms, jokes, puns, etc.

Stages in speech sound development

( ) = sound just beginning to appear, but inconsistent.

Stage	Sounds involving lips	Sounds involving tongue	Sounds at back of mouth
1 1½–2 years	m p b w	n t d	
2 2–2½ years	m p b w	n t d	(ing) (k g) h
3 2½–3½ years	m p b f w	n t d s (l) y	ing k g h
4 3½–4 years	m p b f v w	n t d ch j sh s z l (r) y	ing k g h
5 4½+ years	m p b f v w	n t d ch j th sh s z l r y	ing k g h

Sound production development

	50% of children by	90% of children by
p m h n w	1y 6m	3y
b	1y 6m	4y
k g d	2y	4y
t ng	2y	6y
f y	2y 6m	4y
r l	3y	6y
s	3y	6y
sch h	3y 6m	7y
z	4y	7y
j	4y	7y
v	4y	8y
th	4y 6m	7y
th (the)	5y	8y
s (measure)	6y	8y 6m

Appendix 2

First Words – vocabulary to target in mainstream

There is an overwhelming wealth of vocabulary that young children are expected to know and to understand; most children will gradually increase their vocabulary with very little direct input. Try and select key vocabulary for each curriculum area.

Children with speech and language impairment, however, will also need:

- Consistent terminology to start with and maybe for a considerable time. For example use **plus** until the child is very secure with the concept of addition then gradually introduce other terms or use **Great Britain**, mentioning United Kingdom and the British Isles, but expect the child just to remember and use Great Britain at first.
- Direct teaching of key vocabulary through first-hand multi-sensory experience (visual, auditory, kinaesthetic) whenever possible, then regular revisiting through good photos (digital cameras are great for this) or good pictures, maybe as a personal reference sheet or dictionary.
- Provide as much exposure to the target vocabulary as possible – stories, poems, nursery rhymes, wall charts, videos, sequencing photos or pictures, picture and/or word matching, jigsaws, computer games.
- Careful introduction of new vocabulary – not too much too fast – and try to link it to what the child already knows; help the child to make the connections. Use multi-sensory teaching and have reference chart ready to prompt.

Basic vocabulary

It is often assumed children know this basic vocabulary; however, this may not be the case for children with SLI. The group or set terms, like 'vehicles', 'people' or 'food', will also need to be known and understood. A pupil needs to know and understand the names for individual items and also the group to which they belong, e.g. individual vehicle names – car, plane, bike, train, etc. and the group name 'vehicles'. A pupil is then able to sort items into groups and also to give a group name for a set of items.

In my language resource class this forms the basis of our first words programme because it underpins much curriculum work and because everyday classroom instructional language includes a range of this vocabulary, particularly questions, some verbs and some positions.

Basic vocabulary will be highlighted in bold when it appears under later curriculum headings so that it is easier to select key words which it is really important and helpful to know and understand.

Adjectives - same/different big/little long/short tall/short fat/thin thin/thick wide/narrow heavy/light full/empty deep/shallow noisy, loud/quiet high/low hard/soft wet/dry hot/cold rough/smooth sharp/ blunt silky furry squashy stretchy jerky/smooth dirty/clean pretty/ lovely/ugly nice/awful shiny/dull

Comparatives - 'er'/'est' bigger/smaller biggest/smallest

Adverbs - noisily, loudly/quietly, softly coldly roughly/smoothly quickly, slowly sharply, jerkily/smoothly deeply cleanly strongly/ weakly loosely/tightly kindly/unkindly cleverly/stupidly carefully/ dangerously happily/sadly energetically excitedly

Animals
Pets - cat dog fish bird rabbit mouse
Garden - butterfly caterpillar worm snail ladybird spider bird
Farm - horse cow chicken pig sheep duck goat
Zoo - monkey bear polar bear elephant lion tiger zebra snake giraffe seal
Parts - tail whiskers tusk paws claws beak wings horn
Babies - foal piglet calf chick duckling lamb kitten puppy
Homes - stable pigsty field barn pond hutch tank nest hive hole

Body parts - head hair face eyes nose ears mouth lips teeth tongue neck cheeks shoulders arm hand fingers thumbs leg elbow feet toes knee tummy/stomach chest back wrist ankle nostrils eyelashes eyebrows skin knuckles

Buildings
House - Rooms - kitchen lounge/sitting room bathroom bedroom toilet hall study
Parts - wall door window floor ceiling
Furniture - bed lamp/light cupboard shelves settee/sofa chair table television/telly/TV cooker/oven sink toilet bath mat/rug/carpet curtain heater/fire
Eating - cup saucer knife fork spoon plate dish/bowl teapot jug pan/ saucepan
Things - book balloon blocks/bricks jigsaw puppet doll purse torch telephone clock key comb nailbrush hairbrush dustpan broom needle box bag/carrier bag candle match kettle toaster bucket cushion soap towel toothbrush toothpaste duvet/quilt pillow

School - classroom hall canteen yard/playground tray peg pen pencil felt tip crayon scissors pencil teacher head dinner lady secretary cook caretaker cleaner Nursery Reception Year 1 Year 2 (staff names)

Other buildings - shop supermarket swimming baths/pool zoo castle church garage hospital library railway station police station ambulance station fire station museum cinema lighthouse flats office detached/semi-detached/terraced house bungalow tent

Clothes - pants vest shirt tie socks tee-shirt tights trousers shorts skirt dress jumper shoes pumps trainers coat hat scarf gloves
Fastenings - zip buckle hooks buttons Velcro laces belt
PE kit - pumps/plimsolls/tennis shoes swimsuit/trunks

Colours - red orange yellow green blue black white purple pink grey brown silver gold dark/light darker/lighter shades

Days, months and seasons - Sunday Monday Tuesday Wednesday Thursday Friday Saturday January February March April May June July August September October November December spring summer autumn winter year

Feelings - happy/sad cross, angry, good/naughty bad hungry thirsty tired excited worried surprised afraid scared frightened

Drink - milk juice lemonade pop Coke tea coffee

Food
Fruit - apple banana orange pear strawberry lemon plum grape raspberry blackberry tangerine/satsuma pineapple
Salad - tomato lettuce pepper cress cucumber
Vegetable - potato cabbage onion carrot beans peas
Meat - chicken sausage burger
Other - cheese bread butter biscuit cracker rice spaghetti jelly ice-cream
Christmas food - turkey Christmas pudding Christmas cake mince pie

Jobs - doctor nurse dentist painter plumber artist author musician conductor racing/bus-driver pilot carpenter mechanic actor shop/factory worker zookeeper

Numbers - 1 2 3 4 5 6 7 8 9 10

People/family - Mum Dad boy girl baby man woman people family brother sister friend gran/nana/nan grandad twins cousin aunt uncle nephew niece

Positions - in on under behind in front open/shut, closed up/down top/bottom over off out next to/by between against far/near corner/ middle/edge left/right along forwards/backwards sideways through across above/below back/front upstairs/downstairs at to from about beside together around apart towards/away from inside/outside into/ out of opposite/facing anywhere/everywhere/nowhere/somewhere here where there

Question words - what who where which when why how

Regular questions & directions - What are you going to do? What could you try next? How did you work it out? What do you think? What might happen next? Think of a sensible/good idea. Make a good guess

Shapes - circle square rectangle triangle dot star

Vehicles
Road - car bus van lorry bike scooter motorbike ambulance fire engine police car tractor
Rail - train
Air - plane jet helicopter rocket
Water - boat ship submarine raft yacht hovercraft
Parts - door window seat seatbelt lights wings wheel steering-wheel propeller siren

Verbs - run walk jump skip hop cry laugh sleep wake up drink eat work play stand/sit fall lie down read write dance swim paint draw get pick up hold make cut stick, glue wash dry look listen think act out ask tell balance blow suck break mend bring take build buy sell call carry drop catch throw change choose clap climb come go count cover dig dive empty explain fill fight find lose finish start fly follow forget/remember go/wait give/take grow have hear help hide show hit hurry hurt join keep kick kill kneel knit knock know leave learn teach like love meet mix pay point post pour put pull push pretend ride say see send sew sing shout whisper smell stay start stop tell thank try turn want watch wear win work out use

Weather - sun rain wind snow frost cloudy ice sleet hail thunder lightning storm rainbow dew moon stars earth hot warm cool cold

Additional vocabulary for Key Stage 1, under curriculum headings

Terms are highlighted in **bold** if they have already appeared under basic vocabulary so that it is easier to select key words which are really important and helpful to know and understand.

Art and design

A range of the basic vocabulary will appear in art and design tasks, particularly colours, shapes, feelings, positions; some adjectives and verbs and some materials vocabulary from the science list.

artist designer paint print collage rubbings collection weave tear fold cut join mix match squeeze pinch clay pen pencil felt pen crayon charcoal paint paper card tissue paper crepe paper sticky paper selotape Velcro paper-clip staple wheel axle joint

English

All the basic vocabulary above appears in stories and a range of writing and comprehension tasks.

book story **real imaginary** poem nursery rhyme pictures/ illustrations author write **read beginning middle end** character **who what where when what next** diary list notice page **top bottom left right** alphabet capital lower case letters rhyme syllables sentence full stop word plural spell **talk listen act out start finish** organize check read through **lines shape space join**

Adverbs – noisily loudly/quietly softly coldly roughly smoothly quickly slowly sharply jerkily/smoothly deeply cleanly strongly/weakly loosely/tightly kindly/unkindly cleverly/stupidly carefully/dangerously happily/sadly energetically excitedly

Geography

Position vocabulary underpins all geography work.

Some of the basic vocabulary forms part of geography work, particularly clothes, vehicles, food, buildings, weather and question and direction words.

garden grass flower woods forest **tree** bushes weeds leaf gate fence hedge smoke bonfire pond lake river/stream hill mountain puddle sky cloud park slide swing roundabout climbing frame seaside sea sand bucket spade flag donkey ice-cream funfair

country town city Great Britain Wales England Scotland Ireland map globe atlas

History

Time vocabulary underpins all history work.

Some of the other basic vocabulary will be used when children are being history detectives and looking for things that are the same and are different, particularly clothes, vehicles, food, buildings and question and direction words.

past present

ICT

A range of the basic vocabulary will appear in ICT tasks.
computer screen mouse toolbar programme find record information Roamer tape recorder/cassette player CD player

Mathematics

A range of the basic vocabulary will appear in mathematics tasks, particularly people, animals, vehicles, food, clothes, colours, question and position words and a number of verbs.

Numbers – 12345678910 1st 2nd ... to 10th none nought/zero count count on count back first next last more any more some many more no more too many how many more another most less/fewer too few how many less? least, fewest how much? how many just over/just under enough a little bit a lot all of it some the rest only as much as as many as equals all together a pair twice both double sort group set part whole half quarter

Space in on under behind in front open/shut/closed up/ down top/bottom over off out next to/by between against far/near corner/middle/edge left right along forwards/ backwards sideways through across above/below back/ front at to from about beside together around apart towards/away from inside/outside into/out of opposite/ facing anywhere/everywhere/nowhere/somewhere here where there turn half-turn quarter-turn

Shapes – circle square rectangle triangle dot star straight/ curved line oval diamond hexagon pentagon sphere cube cuboid pyramid cone side face edge point

Measures – big/little long/short tall/short fat/thin thin/ thick wide/narrow heavy/light full/empty deep/shallow weigh balance holds

Time – days names of days today/yesterday/tomorrow **month/ names of the months year seasons** weekend before after how long minutes/hours o'clock half-past quarter to quarter past before/ after afterwards fast/slow early/late now later then evening/night/day old/new old/young once suddenly again sometime long ago while already until always yet soon since almost nearly usually often o'clock/half past, etc. dinner/home/play time

Money – names of all coins coin money how much? spend/spent change price

Music

A range of the basic vocabulary will appear in songs and hymns and to describe how we play (adverbs, feelings), how we feel about music (feelings} and where we hold and play instruments (positions).

play tap bang shake scrape tune **blow** instruments claves shakers drum bells tambour tambourine one sound several sounds silence long/short fast/slow high/low loud/quiet loud/soft rhythm beat pattern repeated pattern

PE

A range of the basic vocabulary will appear in PE tasks, particularly positions, body parts, clothes, colours, shapes, feelings, question words and a number of verbs.

hall field yard space **ball** football tennis cricket chase/tag ring games race sports day hoop quoit rope jumping table bench climbing frame large apparatus changes heart beat pulse blood brain

run walk jump skip hop stand sit fall lie down dance swim get pick up hold make look listen think ask tell bring take build carry drop catch throw change clap climb come go count finish start follow remember go wait give take grow have hear help hide show hit hurry keep kick kneel knock know leave learn teach like meet point post put pull push pretend ride say see send stay start stop try turn want watch wear win use

noisily loudly/quietly softly roughly smoothly quickly slowly sharply jerkily/smoothly deeply strongly/weakly loosely/tightly kindly/unkindly carefully/dangerously happily/sadly energetically excitedly

RE and PSHE

A range of the basic vocabulary will appear in RE and PSHE tasks, particularly feelings, people, animals, food, clothes, colours, question words and a number of verbs.

Church service pray prayer believe Bible hymn cross Christmas Easter and words from other main religions for Year 2s.

Science

A range of the basic vocabulary will appear in science tasks, particularly people, animals, food, clothes, colours, question and direction words and a number of verbs.

same/different noisy, loud/quiet high/low hard/soft wet/dry hot/cold rough/smooth sharp/blunt silky furry squashy stretchy jerky/smooth deep/shallow dirty/clean pretty/lovely/ugly nice/awful shiny/dull plastic/metal/wood/glass/fabric, natural/man-made, see-through [transparent]/not see-through, magnetic/ not magnetic, electricity, circuit, battery, waterproof, strong/weak, push/pull, living/not living/dead, move/bend, twist, stretch, melt, freeze, right/wrong broken/mended tidy/untidy loose/tight sweet/sour seed plant exercise healthy medicine plant **grow** light water **sun rain**

Senses - sight hearing taste touch smell sound fainter quieter/louder

Comparatives – 'er' 'est'

Adverbs – noisily loudly/quietly softly coldly roughly/ smoothly quickly/slowly sharply, jerkily/smoothly deeply cleanly strongly/weakly loosely/tightly kindly/unkindly cleverly/stupidly carefully/dangerously happily/sadly energetically excitedly

Appendix 3 Rhymes

Learning and reciting rhymes can help with:

- developing memory skills;
- articulating particular sounds;
- using expression;
- using a loud enough voice for a group/class to hear;
- curriculum work – some of the rhymes that follow are associated with Key Stage 1 topic or curriculum work, particularly history.

Whichever particular speech sounds your pupils are working on with their speech and language therapist, be ready to praise them for a good attempt. As confidence and skill increase, expect and then praise a better attempt. For instance, if your pupil is working on /b/ then you might expect a clear /b/ at the end of /rub/ or scrub but not expect a clear /r/ or /scr/ as these are harder and will not have been practised yet. Awareness of your pupil's speech programme and of the stages of speech and language development (Appendix 1) is really helpful.

Making up alliterative phrases and sentences can be good fun, as well as providing good speaking practice. For older children, it can form part of writing and spelling tasks.

Silly Susan saw a show on Saturday.
Clever Colin caught a catfish.
Mighty Mouse made a mantrap.

Some of the rhymes we use are listed on the following pages. Some are at a simple level; others are harder with the target sound in different positions. A wider selection is given in *Phonic Rhyme Time* by Mary Nash-Wortham (LDA).

B

Bee, Bee
A bee on me!
Bzzzz

I rub and I rub
At the tub, tub, tub.
My dirty clothes
I scrub, scrub, scrub.

Bl

Black and blue
Black and blue
How are you?
I'm black and blue.

Br

New brooms!
New brooms!
Buy my brooms
to brush your rooms.
New brooms!

C

Come and play
Come and play
Can you come to my house today?

Ch

Chip chop, chip chop, chip chop Joe.
Chip chop, chip chop, chip chop Joe.
One big blow,
Ouch my toe!
Chip chop, chip chop, chip chop Joe.

Cl

Clip clop! Clip clop!
Go and never stop
Gee up my little pony
Clip clop! Clip clop!

Cr

Crash!
Don't be cross Mum, Don't be cross.
It was an accident.
Don't be cross Mum, Don't be cross.

D

Oh dear! Oh dear!
Poor Dan
Oh dear!

Have you heard about our Neddy?
Poor Ned, Poor Ned.
Have you heard about our Neddy?
Dead, dead, dead.

Dr

Careful with your drink
Don't you spill a drop
Careful with your drink
Don't let it drip, drip, drop.

F

Jeremiah blow the fire puff, puff, puff.
Blow it gently f f f
Blow it rough fff fff fff
Jeremiah blow the fire puff, puff, puff.

Fl

There is a fly I know there is
I saw it on the floor
There is a fly I know there is
I heard it by the door.
Zzzzzzzzzzzzzzzzzzzz

Fr

5 little frogs sitting on a well
1 leaned over and down he fell
Frogs jump high
Frogs jump low
4 little frogs jump to and fro.

4 little frogs sitting on a well...

G

Go, go, go
Go fast not slow
Go, go, go

There was a little dog and he had a little tail.
And he used to wag, wag, wag it.
But if he was sad or if he'd been bad.
Then he would drag, drag, drag it.

Gl

Glory! Glory!
I'm SO glum
I'll sit and look sad and suck my thumb.
Glory! Glory!
I'm SO glad
I'll run very fast to meet my Dad.

Gr

These are Grandma's glasses.
[Put fingers round eyes]
This is Grandma's hat.
[Put hands on head in hat shape]
Grandma claps her hands like this
And folds them in her lap.
These are Grandad's glasses.
[Put fingers round eyes]
This is Grandad's hat.
[Put hands on head in hat shape]
Grandad folds his arms liks this
And has a little nap.

H

Here's a pieman
Hi! Hi! Hi!
Here's a penny
For a hot, hot pie.

J

Here I am little jumping Joan
Jump, jump, jump
When nobody's with me I'm all alone
Jump, jump, jump.

L

Look out! Look out!
A car is coming.
Look out! Look out!
A car is coming.
Here it comes going so fast
Just stand back and let it past.
Look out! Look out!
A car is coming.

M

Me, me, me
Give it to me
Me, me, me
Please

My motor is humming
I'm coming, I'm coming
Make room, make room, make room!
Not a minute to wait,
I'm late, late, late,
Make room, make room, make room!

N

No, no, no
Off you go
No, no, no

All night long when the wind is high.
Nnn Nnn Nnn Nnn
The lightships moan and moan to the sky.
The foghorns whine as the fog runs free
Warning the men in the ships at sea.
Nnn Nnn Nnn Nnn

P

Pie, pie
I love pie
Pie, pie
Mmmmm!

Pease pudding hot
Pease pudding cold
Pease pudding in the pot
Nine days old.

Pl

Please, please, please mum.
Plenty of peas Mum
Plenty of peas Mum
Please, please, please.

Pr

Prick your finger princess.
Prick your finger so.
Prick your finger princess.
And off to sleep you go.

Q

Queenie, Queenie, who's got the ball?
Are they short or are they tall?
Are they fat or are they thin?
Queenie, Queenie, who will win?

(This is a ball game where one child [Queenie] stands with her back to the rest who stand in a line. Queenie throws the ball over her shoulder and one child catches it and hides it behind her back. All children put hands behind backs. Queenie turns round and they say rhyme to her, she then guesses who's got the ball – if right has another go and if wrong the child with the ball becomes Queenie.)

R

Turn rope turn.
Round and round
High in the air
And down on the ground
Turn rope turn.
Round and round.

S

A sailor went to sea, sea, sea
To see what he could see, see, see
But all that he could see, see, see
Was the bottom of the deep blue sea,
sea, sea.

Sc/Sk

Here's your scarf and here's your hat
Off to school you go
Here's your bag now scat! scat! scat!
Off to school you go.

Sh

Shoe shine! Shoe shine! Shouts the
shoe shine boy.
Shoe shine! Shoe shine! Shouts the
shoe shine boy.
Shine your shoes sir!
Shine your shoes sir!
Shoe shine! Shoe shine! Shouts the
shoe shine boy.

Sl

Slugs, slugs slide so slow
Leaving silver tracks wherever they go.

Sm

If the smoke is black
Alas! Alack!
If the smoke is grey
It'll be a nice day.

Sn

Snow, snow glorious snow
On our sledges down we go
On the snow snow glorious snow.

Sp

I saw a spider spinning a web
I saw a spider crawling up the wall
I saw a spider in a sunny spot
Then he wasn't there at all.

St

The policeman's standing still in
the street
Stopping the cars just standing on
his feet
STOP! STOP! STOP!

Sw

Sweep, sweep, sweep
Sweep with your broom
Sweep, sweep, sweep
Sweep all of the room.

T

Our great church clock goes TICK TOCK TICK TOCK.
Our sitting room clock goes Tick-tack Tick-tack Tick-tack.
My little watch goes ticker-tacker, ticker-tacker, ticker-tacker.

Th

What a thing!/I have to choose
This one or that one, that one or this
I want both but I can't have both.
This one or that one I have to choose.

Tr

Trip trap, trip trap all the way to town
Trip trap, trip trap bouncing all around.
It's not a comfy way to ride
Bouncing about from side to side
Trip trap, trip trap all the way to town.

Tw

Twenty-two and twenty-four
Twist the handle, open the door
Twenty-six and twenty-eight
Run inside I just can't wait.

V

If you ever, ever, ever see a whale
You must never, never tread upon its tail.
For if you ever, ever tread upon its tail.
You will never live to see another whale.

W

Where does the flame on the candle go
when you blow it out? I would like to know.
Where does it come from and where does it go?
That is what I would like to know.

Y

Yawning [ ] is a sight
He yawns and yawns with all his might
He yawns all day and he yawns all night
Yawning, yawning [ ]

(Put in each child's name in turn and use he or she as appropriate.)

Z

Buzz, buzz, buzz went the busy, busy bee.
Buzz, buzz, buzz, buzz, buzz went he.

Acknowledgements:

It is impossible to give the source of all the rhymes included here. Some were jotted down while the author was searching for material for lessons. Others have been passed down orally. Every effort has been made to trace and acknowledge copyright owners. Apologies are offered to any author or copyright holder whose rights have been unintentionally infringed and due acknowledgement will be made in subsequent editions on notification being made to the publishers.

The rhymes for the following letters - B, Bl, Br, C, Cl, Cr, F, Fl, Fr, G, Gl, L, M, N, P, S, Sn, St, Sw, T, Tw, W, Y and Z - have been made up by the author or are taken or adapted from rhymes in *Speech Rhymes* edited by Clive Sansom, A & C Black (1975) ISBN 0 7136 1425 0

'Chip chop Joe' and 'These are Grandma's glasses' are taken from *This Little Puffin* compiled by Elizabeth Matterson, Penguin (1969)

'Five little frogs' is taken from *One, Two, Three, Four - Number Rhymes and Finger Games* by Mary Grice, Frederick Warne (1974)

'There was a little dog' is taken from *I Never Saw A Purple Cow and other Nonsense Rhymes* by Emma Chichester Clark, Walker Books (1990)

'Here I am little Jumping Joan' is taken from *Lavender's Blue - A Book of Nursery Rhymes* OUP, London (1967)

'Turn rope turn' is taken from a poem by John Agard in *Playtime Rhymes* selected by John Foster, OUP (1998)

The rhymes on page 9 are from *165 Chants for Children.* Edited by Mary Lou Colgin, Gryphon House Publishing (1992) and *A Child's Treasury of Milligan,* Spike Milligan, Virgin Publishing (2000)

Appendix 4 Questions

I keep six honest serving men
They taught me all I knew;
Their names are What and Why and When
And How and Where and Who.

(From 'The Elephant's Child' in *Just So Stories* by Rudyard Kipling, Everyman Library Children's Classics, 1992)

Some children have a lot of difficulty in answering and, particularly, *asking* questions. Even children without recognized speech and language difficulties can stumble when asked to devise appropriate questions. It is a skill that must be taught and practised.

At the same time, adults can find it hard to ask open-ended questions. Teachers, especially, may ask a question knowing exactly the answer they want to hear from the child. When that answer is not forthcoming, they can be reluctant to accept alternatives, casting round the group until they get the 'nearest match' to the answer in their own mind, or giving up and 'putting the words into the mouths' of pupils.

It may be helpful to script questions to match the curriculum area or bank of vocabulary being worked on. Build up a bank of encouraging responses to children who have a go, but get it wrong:

'That's an interesting idea ...'
'Well tried, Jason, you're on the right lines ...'
'Mmm, can anyone add something else to what Poppy has said?'
'I need to think about that ...'
'Thank you for that answer, Darius. Let's try and work out how you got to it. Remember, the question was ...'

Teachers will be familiar with the strategy of naming the child, before asking the question, so that he is 'cued-in' and attentive. 'Kevin, can you tell us ...?' It is a useful approach to share with parents.

There is an order of difficulty in questioning. **What**, **where** and **who** are usually easier than **when**, **how** and **why**. However, any kind of 'What if?' question or one that uses 'might', 'could' or 'would' is more abstract and may be as difficult as a 'Why' question.

Answering and asking questions is an important part of all curriculum work and indeed an essential life skill. The examples that follow focus on questions that may arise in design and technology work.

What?

What is it called?
What does it smell/taste/feel/sound/look like?
What size/colour is it?
What decoration does it have/what does the decoration tell you?
What lettering is there?
What is it made from/what raw materials made that?
What could be used instead of it?
What is worth to you/to a sale room/to a man marooned on a desert island?

Where?

Where was it used/designed/made/disposed of?
Where did the museum get it from/the designer get the idea from/the materials come from?
Where would it be of most value/you keep it?
Where could you get another?

Who?

Who designed/used/made/likes/threw it away?
Who else has got one/wants one?
Who would buy it now/choose it?
Who might have bought it when it was new?

When?

When was it designed/made/used/obsolete/disposed of/altered?
When would you find it useful?

How?

How was it made/designed?
How does it work/the material affect the shape/it reflect society's attitudes or culture?
How well made/designed is it?
How well does it work?
How can it be improved/replaced?
How could it be better designed?
How would it have been made 100 years ago/you feel using it every day?
How many of them are there?

Why?

Why is it this size/shape/colour/material?
Why does it have this lettering/decoration?
Why was it made?
Why is no longer used?
Why would anyone pay a lot of money for it?

Appendix 5 Word Banks

The following pages may be photocopied and used to make a word-bank book. The word wall is produced as a blank copy on page 171 for you to write in fewer and/or different words as appropriate. Again, pupils will use this, so it should be an easy-to-read font like comic sans.

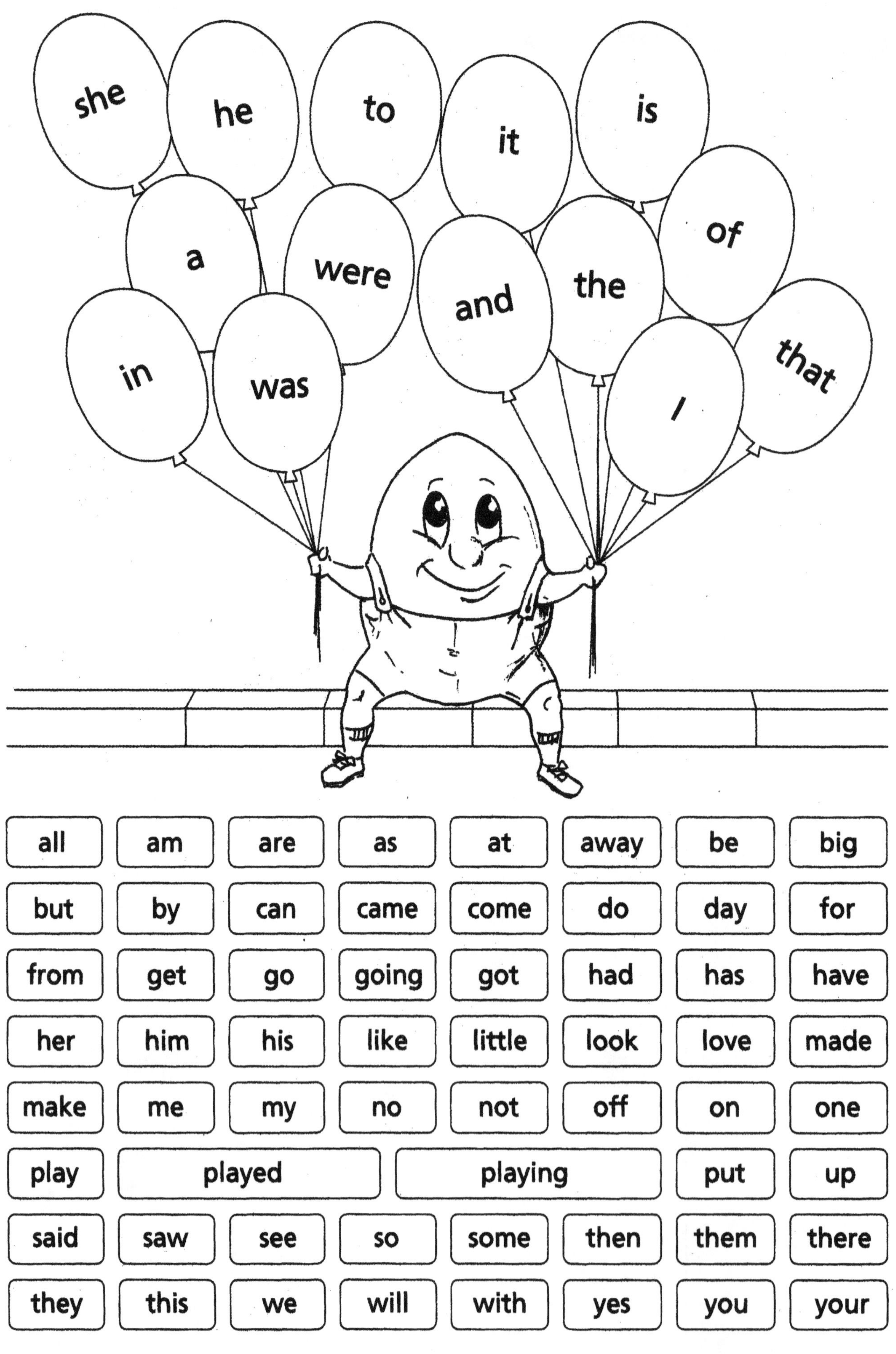
she
he
to
it
is
a
were
and
the
of
in
was
I
that
all am are as at away be big
but by can came come do day for
from get go going got had has have
her him his like little look love made
make me my no not off on one
play played playing put up
said saw see so some then them there
they this we will with yes you your

giant	monster	dragon	witch	old woman
old man	dinosaur	little boy	little girl	cat
dog	ghost	robot	queen	king
princess	prince	house	cottage	castle
palace	cave	volcano	one	red
			two	orange
			three	yellow
			four	green
			five	blue
hole	tent	tree house	six	pink
			seven	purple
			eight	black
			nine	white
			ten	brown
			lots	grey
			hundred	silver
			more	gold
			not many	blond

big little	fat thin	rich poor	happy sad cross	lonely friend	beautiful handsome ugly
Once One day Once upon a time		there		was lived	

garden
house
bike
ball
rope
park
trees
swing
roundabout
duck
slide
seesaw
shop
supermarket
SUPERMART
town
bought
sweets
crisps
school
teacher
friends
zoo
animals
fair
seaside
water
sand
bucket
spade
ice cream
watched television
computer
tea
bed
home

Aa	
Bb	
Cc	
Ch ch	
Dd	
Ee	
Ff	
Gg	
Hh	
Ii	
Jj	
Kk	
Ll	
Mm	
Nn	

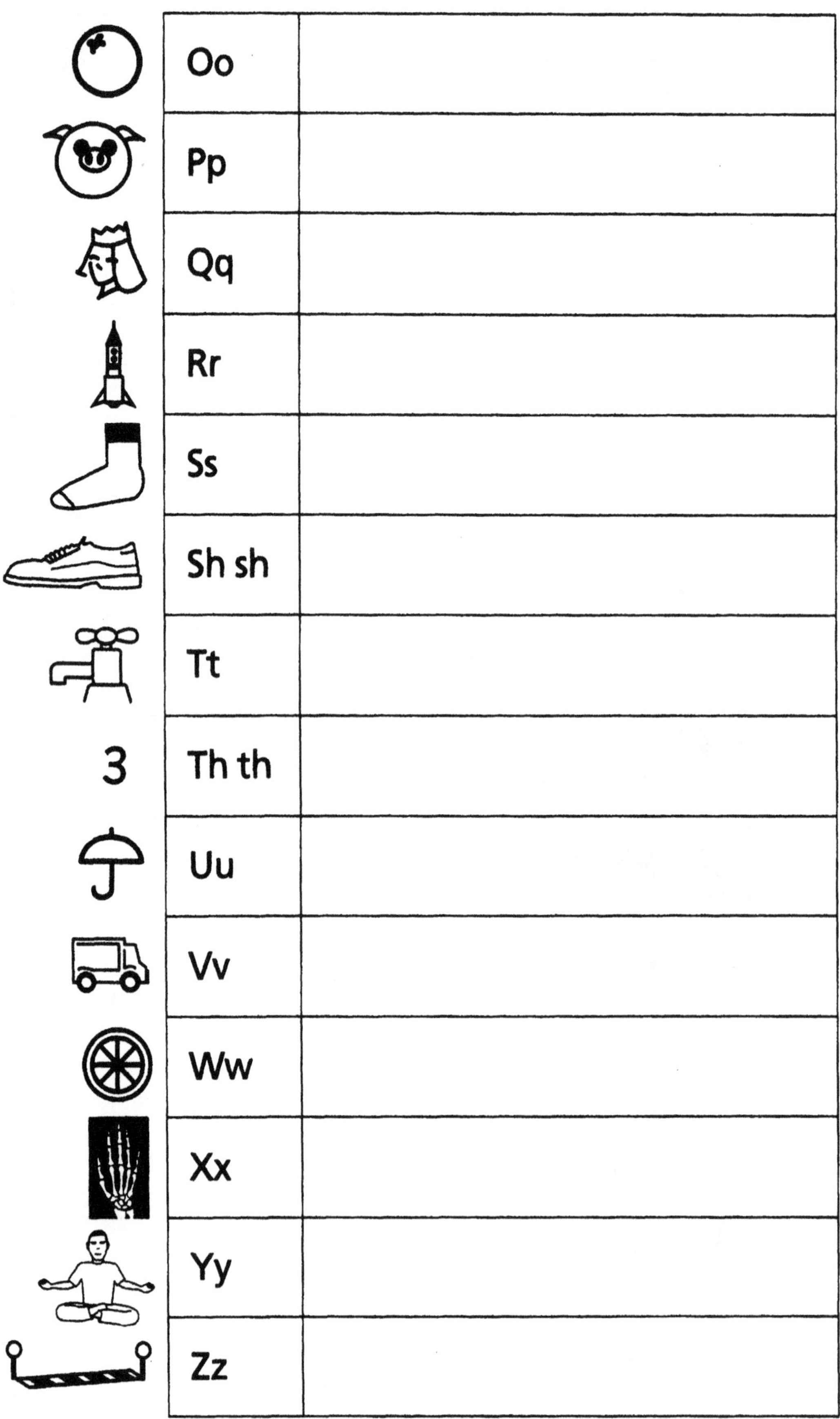

Oo	
Pp	
Qq	
Rr	
Ss	
Sh sh	
Tt	
Th th	
Uu	
Vv	
Ww	
Xx	
Yy	
Zz	

Calendars

Appendix 6

Construct a simple calendar that a child could use at home, use Blu-tack to move the yesterday/today/tomorrow along. Put in personal key events – school days and home days, Rainbows, swimming, etc.

Some children may need the calendar broken down into the 'number of sleeps' rather than, or as well as, the days, so draw in a sun and a bed on each day.

Monday	Tuesday	Wednesday	Thursday	Friday	Saturday	Sunday

Yesterday	Today	Tomorrow

As children become confident, a more detailed version can be used. Draw in the events, especially ones for which equipment from home has to be taken into school – recorders, PE, swimming, etc.

	Monday	Tuesday	Wednesday	Thursday	Friday	Saturday	Sunday
Morning breakfast							
Afternoon lunch							
Evening tea							

It may be useful to have a whole-year calendar that is on view all the time. Put in special events such as birthdays and Christmas, etc.

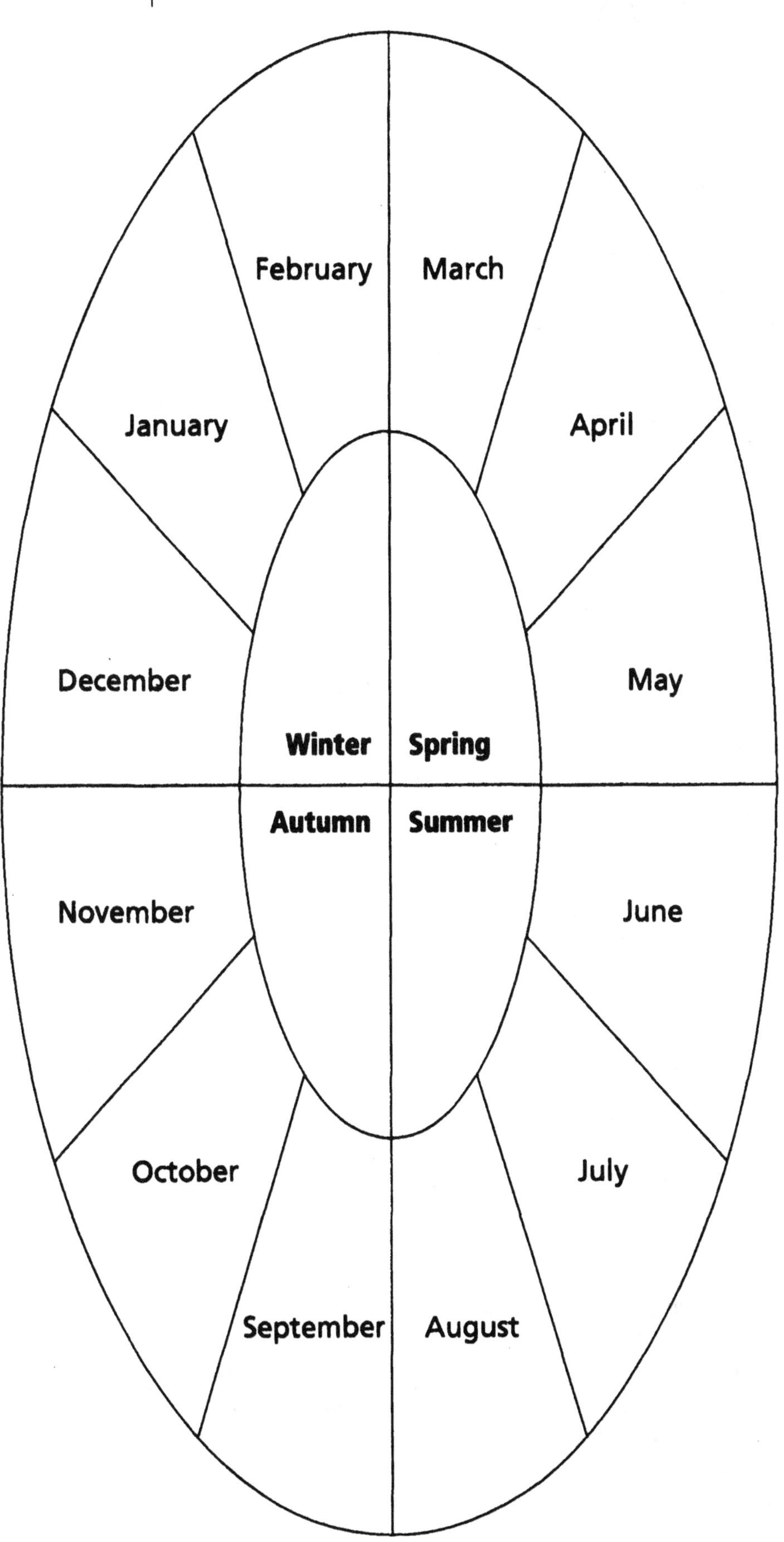

References and Resources

Introduction

Books/References

Donaldson, M. (1995) *Children and Language Impairments: An Introduction*, Jessica Kingsley, London.
JPDF – Joint Professional Development Foundation level course from ICAN, 4 Dyers Buildings, Holborn, London EC1N 2QU or online at www.ican.org.uk
Pinker, S. (1994) *The Language Instinct: The New Science of Language and Mind*, Penguin Science, Harmondsworth.

1. What is Speech and Language Impairment?

Books/References

Hall, D.M.B. (1996) *Health for all Children: A Programme for Child Health Surveillance* (3rd edn), Oxford University Press, Oxford.
Johnson, M. *Functional Language in the Classroom*, available from the Department of Psychology and Speech Pathology, Manchester Metropolitan University, Elizabeth Gaskell site, Hathersage Road, Manchester M13 0JA.
Law, J., Lindsay, G., Peacey, N., Gascoigne, M., Soloff, N., Radford, J., Band, S. and Fitzgerald, L. (2000) *Provision for Children with Speech and Language Needs in England and Wales: Facilitating Communication between Education and Health Services*, DfEE, London.
Stackhouse J. (1997) Unpublished keynote speech at Acton Infant Language Resource SEN Conference.

2. Expressive Language

Books/References

Berry, M. (1980) *Teaching Linguistically Handicapped Children*, Prentice-Hall, Englewood Cliffs, NJ.
Biddulph, L. and McQueen, D. (2001) *How to Help Talking.* From First Community Health, Beecroft Clinic, Cannock Chase Hospital, Brunswick Road, Cannock, Staffordshire, WS11 2XY.
Cooke, J. and Williams, D. (1985) *Working with Children's Language*, Winslow Press, Bicester.

Dodd, B. (1994) *Differential Diagnosis and Treatment of Speech Disordered Children,* Whurr, Chichester.
Hutt, E. (1986) *Teaching Language Disordered Children,* Arnold, London.
Martin, D. and Miller, C. (1996) *Speech and Language Difficulties in the Classroom,* David Fulton, London.
Mogford, K. and Sadler, J. (1995) *Child Language Disability: Implications in an Educational Setting,* Egghead Publications, Clevedon.
Moodley, M. and Reynell, J. (1978) *Helping Language Development,* Arnold, London.
Snowling, M. and Stackhouse, J. (1995) *Dyslexia, Speech and Language: A Practitioner's Book,* Whurr, Chichester.
Turnbull, J. and Stewart, T. (1995) *Helping Children Cope with Stammering,* Sheldon Press, Lincoln.

Resources

- **AFASIC**
  2nd floor, 50–52 Great Sutton Street, London EC1V 0DJ.
  This is a parent-led organization that works on behalf of children and young people who have a speech and language difficulty. AFASIC publishes a number of useful leaflets and booklets.
- **Black Sheep Press**
  67 Middleton, Cowling, Keighley, W. Yorks BD22 0DQ or online at www.blacksheep-epress.com
  An extensive range of reasonably priced and photocopiable language materials.
- **Bullying and the Dysfluent Child in Primary School (1992)**
  From The British Stammering Association, 15 Old Ford Road, London E2 9PJ.
- ***Class Talk*** by Rosemary Sage
  Network Educational Press Ltd, PO Box 635, Stafford ST16 1BF.
  This has a useful Communication Skills Rating and a range of language games for older pupils.
- ***Earwiggo*** by Jan Holdstock (1984)
  Lovely Music, 17 Westgate, N. Yorks LS24 9JB.
  A set of six books on rhythm, pitch and simple songs.
- **Early Learning Centre**
  The high street shop sells a range of small-world toys most useful for language work and we have found their What Do I Use game useful too.
- ***Foundations of Literacy*** by Sue Palmer and Ros Bayley (2004)
  Network Educational Press, Stafford.
  A balanced approach to language, listening and literacy skills in the early years. Rooted in oracy with a wealth of practical suggestions.
- ***Functional Language in the Classroom*** by Maggie Johnson
  Available from the Department of Psychology and Speech Pathology, Manchester Metropolitan University, Elizabeth Gaskell site, Hathersage Road, Manchester M13 0JA.
  Ideas and suggestions to improve listening and understanding.

- **Joint Professional Development Foundation** (2001) (ICAN) www.ican.org.uk
  I CAN offers a structure for continuing professional development in speech, language and communication impairment. It is endorsed by the Department for Education and Skills, the Royal College of Speech and Language Therapists, Department of Health and the Teacher Training Agency. It is a common framework for the continuing professional development of teachers and speech and language therapists.
- ***Language Development: Circle Time Sessions to Improve Communication Skills*** by Marion Nash, Jackie Lowe and Tracey Palmer, (2002) published by David Fulton, London.
  There are now companion books for mathematics and science; sessions are set out and are easy to follow or to dip into. Particular vocabulary and language concepts are covered with inbuilt repetition.
- ***The Language Gap*** by S. Gowers and E. Sisson (1995)
  Available from SENTER, Freepost NT 2550, Whitley Bay NE26 1BR. Photocopiable games and pictures for language development (auditory memory, verbal reasoning, sequencing).
- **Lawrence Educational**
  17 Redruth Road, Walsall, West Midlands WS5 3EJ or online at www.educationalpublications.com, for Beat baby and rap books.
- **LDA**
  Duke Street, Wisbech, Cambs PE13 2AE or online at www.instructionalfair.co.uk
  A wide range of resources to support speech and language work. We have found Sound Beginnings - a phonological awareness pack - and LDA Language cards, especially Social Sequences and Actions cards, particularly useful.
- ***Living Language*** and ***Teaching Talking*** by Ann Locke (1991)
  NFER Nelson, 2 Oxford Road East, Windsor, Berks SL4 1DF or online at edu&hsc@nfer-nelson.co.uk
- **Orchard Toys**
  Formlend Ltd, Keyworth, Nottingham but also available from high street shops. We have found their Quack Quack and Insy Winsy games very useful.
- **Order Order**
  Photocopiable sequencing sheets available from Easy Learn, Trent House, Fiskerton, Southwell, Notts NG25 0UH.
- ***PORIC*** by Glinette Woods and Deborah Acors (1999)
  Language Concepts Instruction Book and Books 1–4 and Past Tense and Concept Calendar from Cheerful Publications, 7 Oxley Close, Gidea Park, Romford, Essex RM2 6NX.
- **Questions Publishing**
  1st floor, Leonard House, 321 Bradford Street, Digbeth, Birmingham B5 6ET or online at www.questionsonlinecatalogue.co.uk
- **Ravensburger games**
  Available from high street shops. We have found What's My Name and Tell a Story very useful.

- ***SALLEY*** - Structured Activities for Language and Literacy in the Early Years by Angela Hurd and Diana McQueen (2002)
  A structured programme including listening, language and phonological awareness activities.
- **Secondary Students with Speech and Language Impairment** - Guidance for Inclusion (2001)
  Also 'Primary Students with Speech and Language Impairment - Guidance for Inclusion'.
  Available from Educational Psychology, PO Box 4, County Hall, St Anne's Crescent, Lewes, E. Sussex BN7 1SG.
- **Sequencing stories**
  Photocopiable sequencing material at three levels.
  Available from Learning Materials Ltd, Dixon Street, Wolverhampton WV2 2BX or online at
  Learning.Materials@btinternet.com
- ***Speaking and Listening Games*** by Margaret Curran (2004). Published by Brilliant Publications and available from BEBC Distribution, Albion Close, Parkstone, Poole, Dorset BH12 3LL.
- **Speechmark Publishing**
  A range of books and products.
  Telford Road, Bicester, Oxon OX26 4LQ or online at
  www.speechmark.net
- **STASS**
  44 North Road, Ponteland, Northumberland NE20 9UR.
  A range of resources to support speech and language work including Cued Articulation books, Language Steps - language activities for young children with photocopiable material to make your own games, Semantic Links and Teddy Language Pack
- **Talking Dice (2000)**
  Unit M323, Cardiff Bay Business Centre, Lewis Road, Ocean Park, Cardiff CF24 58S or online at www.talkingdice.co.uk
  A most useful resource for Infant, Junior, Secondary and beyond; these dice can be used to teach and to reinforce vocabulary.
- **Winslow Press**
  Goytside Road, Chesterfield, Derbys. S40 2PH.
  A wide range of resources to support speech and language work including Pictures Please, Pronoun Party Game Board, Mighty Mouth game, Silly Songs for Phonology and Sound Awareness, Colour Cards and Why Do You Do? Set.
- ***Working with Secondary Students with Language Difficulties*** by Mandy Brent, Florence Gough and Susan Robinson (2004). Published by David Fulton, London.

3. Receptive Language

Books

Ebbinghaus, H. (1964) in *Memory: A Contribution to Experimental Psychology*, H. A. Ruger and C. E. Brussenis, New York Teacher's College, Columbia University. (Original work published 1885.)

Reynell, J. (1976) *Developmental Language Scales*, NFER/Nelson, Windsor.

Rider, C. (2002) 'Well-being and involvement' in *Special Children* (Feb./Mar.) published by Questions Publishing, 1st floor, Leonard House, 321 Bradford Street, Digbeth, Birmingham B5 6ET or online at www.questionsonlinecatalogue.co.uk

Resources

Many of the books and resources for Expressive language given above contain information and ideas for Receptive language development.

In addition:

- **Lawrence Educational Ltd**
  17 Redruth Road, Walsall, West Midlands WS5 3EJ or online at www.educationalpublications.com for *Helping Young Children to Listen with Lola, Speaking, Listening and Thinking with Dogum, Helping Young Children to Imagine* and *Helping Young Children to Concentrate* by Ros Bayley and Lynn Broadbent (2003).
- **Leap into Listening**
  Photocopiable listening activities, from Winslow, Goytside Road, Chesterfield, Derbys. S40 2PH.
- **Learning Materials Ltd**
  Dixon Street, Wolverhampton WV2 2BX or online at learning.materials@btinternet.com
  Reading for Meaning
  Think about it
  Sound Lotto – various sets
  Listen and Colour
- **Listen and Do**
  From LDA, Duke Street, Wisbech, Cambs. PE13 2AE.
- **Listening Skills Early Years and Listening Skills Key Stage 1 (1994)**
  Photocopiable sheets for listening activities/tasks.
  Available from Questions Publishing.
- **The Little Book of Listening**, by Clare Beswick (2003)
  Featherstone Education Ltd, 44–46 High Street, Husbands Bosworth, Lutterworth, Leics. LE17 6LP
  or online at www.featherstone.uk.com
- ***More Reading for Meaning*** CD-ROM
  From Taskmaster, Morris Road, Leicester LE2 6BR or online at www.taskmasteronline.co.uk
  A set of Good listening, Good thinking, Good waiting, Good talking posters by Maggie Johnson.
- ***My Social Story Book*** by Carol Gray (2001). Published by Jessica Kingsley, London or online at www.thegraycenter.org

- **Questions Publishing**
  1st Floor, Leonard House, 321 Bradford Street, Digbeth, Birmingham B5 6ET or online at www.questionsonlinecatalogue.co.uk for two Listening activity books, one for Early Years and one for Key Stage 1.
- **What am I?**
  Listening game with cassette and cards from Early Learning Centre shops.

4. Social Use of Language Skills and Behaviour

Books/References

Anderson-Wood, L. and Rae Smith, B. (1989) *Working with Pragmatics*, Winslow Press, Chesterfield.

Cohen, N.J., Menna, R., Vallance, D.D., Barwick, M.A., Im, N. and Horodezky, N.M. (1988) 'Language, social cognitive processing and behavioural characteristics of psychiatrically disturbed children with previously unidentified and unsuspected language impairments', *Journal of Child Psychology and Psychiatry* (39)6, 853–64.

Conti-Ramsden, G. and McTear, M. (1992) *Pragmatic Disorders in Children – Assessment and Intervention*, Whurr, Chichester.

Cross, M. (2004) *Children with Emotional and Behavioural Difficulties and Communication Problems: There is Always a Reason* Jessica Kingsley, London.

Donahue, M., Cole, D. and Hartas, D. (1994) 'Links between language and emotional/behavioural disorders', *Education and Treatment of Children* 17, 245–54.

Firth, C. and Venkatesh, K. (1999) *Semantic-Pragmatic Language Disorder Resource Pack*, Winslow Press, Chesterfield.

Gray, C. (2001) *My Social Story Book*, Jessica Kingsley, London, or online at www.thegraycenter.org

Grundy, P. (1995) *Doing Pragmatics*, Arnold, London.

Lucas, E. (1980, rep. 1991) *Semantic Pragmatic Language Disorders*, Aspen, CO.

Martin, D. and Miller, C. (1996) *Speech and Language Difficulties in the Classroom*, David Fulton, London.

Oldham Speech Therapy Department. *Hold my glasses and don't nibble the ends* (A practical guide to working with semantic pragmatic language disordered children), Speech Therapy Dept. Oldham NHS Trust, Oldham.

Rinaldi, W. (1995) *The Social Use of Language Programme (Primary and Pre-school Teaching Pack)*, NFER: Lindsor.

Rustin, L. and Kuhr, A. (1989) *Social Skills and the Speech Impaired*, Whurr, Chichester.

Staskowski, M., Kenney, M.C. and King, C.A. (1994) 'Language disorders and learning disabilities in school-refusing adolescents', *Journal of the American Academy of Child and Adolescent Psychiatry* 33, 1331–7.

Resources

Playground games

Goodwin, J. (1997) *100 Games*, Headstart, London.
James, F. and Brownsword, K. (1994) *A Positive Approach*, Belair, Dunstable.
Mashedr, M. (1991) *Let's Play Together*, Merlin Press, London.
Sher, B. (1995) *Popular Games for Positive Play* Therapy Skill Builders, Psychological Corporation, Tucson, AZ.
Sher, B. (1998) *Self Esteem Games*, John Wiley & Sons, New York.

Circle Time

Bliss, T. and Tetley, J. (1997) *Circle Time* and *Developing Circle Time*, Lucky Duck, Bristol.
Child, P. (2004) *Two Years of Successful Circle Time: A Tried and Tested Programme for Years 1 and 2*, Positive Press, Trowbridge.
Collins, M. (2004) *Circling Safely*, Lucky Duck, Bristol.
Mad, Sad, Glad game (motions photo cards), Winslow, Goytside Road, Chesterfield, Derbys. S40 2PH.
Mortimer, H. (1998) *Learning through Play-Circle Time*, Scholastic, London.
Moseley, J. (1996) *Here We Go Round, Quality Circle Time, More Quality Circle Time*, LDA, Wisbech.
Sonnet, H. and Child, P. (2002) *Stepping Stones to Success: A Two-Year Quality Circle Time Programme for Early Years*, Positive Press, Trowbridge.
The Giggly, Grumpy, Scary Book (a songbook with CD), Universal Edition, London.

A teacher-made toolkit for circle games is useful. Mine includes:

- blindfold
- set of keys
- large foam ball
- magic wand
- soft toy/shell or similar to pass round when talking round the circle
- clear photos/pictures of happy/sad, etc.
- favourite book, toy, colour, food, etc.

A number of companies produce praise/reward badges. I like Superstickers, PO Box 55, 4 Balloo Avenue, Bangor, County Down BT19 7PJ as they have a 'I listen carefully' badge.

In addition, try Praise Postcards, The Primary Print People, 142 Blackburn Road, Bolton, Lancs. BL1 8DR.

And *Celebrations* (2002), a book of photocopiable certificates by George Robinson and Barbara Maines from Lucky Duck Publications, 10 South Terrace, Redland, Bristol BS6 6TG.

5. Developmental Co-ordination and Sensory Difficulties

Books/References

Beattie, L.F.C., *Tips with Teens*, Dyspraxia Foundation, 8 West Alley, Hitchen, Herts. SG5 1EG.

Dennison, P. and Dennison, G. (1989) *Brain Gym*, Body Balance Books, 12 Golders Rise, London NW4 2HR.

Hornsby, B., Shear, F. and Pool, J. (1999) *Alpha to Omega Teacher's Handbook*, Heinemann Educational, Oxford.

Kirby, A. (1999) *Dyspraxia: The Hidden Handicap*, Human Horizon Series.

Kranowitz, C.S. (1998) *The Out of Sync Child*, Berkley Publishing Group, New York.

Macintyre (2000) *Dyspraxia in the Early Years*, David Fulton, London.

Marshall, L., *Handwriting Activities*, from Communications Manager, Education Dept., The Castle, Winchester.

Meister-Vitale, B. (1982) *Unicorns are Real: A Right-brained Approach to Learning*, Jalmer Press, or online at www.personhoodpress.com.

Oakes Park School and Support Service, *Working with Clumsy Children: A Practical Approach for Teachers*, available from Oakes Park School and Support Service, Matthews Lane, Sheffield S8 8JJ.

Poustie, J., *Life Skills: Practical Solutions for Specific Learning Difficulties*, Dyspraxia Foundation or online at www.janpoustie.co.uk

Ripley, K., Daines, B. and Barett, J. (2001) *Inclusion for Children Dyspraxia/DCD: A Handbook for Teachers*, David Fulton, London.

Russell, J.P. (1987) *Graded Activities for Children with Motor Difficulties*, Cambridge University Press, Cambridge.

Supporting the child with dyspraxia in the mainstream classroom, SENSS North Lincolnshire from Mrs P Barthorpe, Head of Service, SENSS, Educational Development Centre, South Leys Campus, Enderby Road, Scunthorpe, N Linc. DN17 2JL.

Witherick, S., *Assessment and Activities for Hand Skills and Fine Motor development - A practical guide for teachers*, ReLeass c/o Educational Services, 10–12 George Hudson Street, York YO1 6ZG.

Resources

- **Anything Left-Handed**
  18 Avenue Road, Belmont, Surrey SM2 6JD.
  A range of resources for left-handers including the Yoropen and a sloping board.
- **Crossbow Educational**
  41 Sawpit Lane, Brocton, Staffs. ST17 0TE or online at www.crossboweducational.com
  A wide range of spelling games and most useful colour filter rulers that can be used to change the background colour while reading.

- **The Dyspraxia Foundation** is a national charity that supports and informs those concerned with Dyspraxia (DCD). It publishes a number of useful leaflets, booklets and books, including a booklet written by parents called Living with Dyspraxia - Handy Tips full of ideas to help children with dyspraxia cope on a day-to-day basis.
- **Easylearn**
  Trent House, Fiskerton, Southwell, Notts. NG25 0UH or online at enquiry@easylearn.co.uk
  A range of useful photocopiable resources including Fine Motoring - photocopiable sheets with a range of fine motor skills.
- **Folk in Education Resources for Schools**
  4 Mill Lane, Much Cowarne, near Bromyard, Herefordshire HR7 4JH.
  Music and dance resources including Fun Folk Dances by Marion Percy - 12 very simple folk dances, some based on nursery rhymes, good for rhythm and for direction, sequencing and learning left and right.
- **Gymnic/Epsan Waterfly UK Ltd**
  Anglo House, Worcester Road, Stourport on Severn, DY13 9AW or online at salesuk@epsanwaterfly.com. Movin'sit posture cushions and many more resources to support the development of co-ordination and movement skills.
- **The Happy Puzzle Company**
  Mail order from PO Box 24041, London NW4 2ZN or online at www.happypuzzle.co.uk
  Puzzles and games, some of which are useful for developing manipulative and motor-planning skills.
- **LDA**
  Duke Street, Wisbech, Cambs. PE13 2AE.
  A range of useful products, including:
    Let's Look - photocopiable visual discrimination sheets
    Lined paper - helpful guidelines for writing
    Write from the Start (formerly Theoderescu) - photocopiable booklets to help develop fine motor and perceptual skills.
    Tri-go grip - the pencil grip we have found to be most effective with right- or left-handers.
- **Philip & Tacey Ltd**
  North Way, Andover, Hants. SP10 5BA.
- **Rompa Ltd**
  Goytside Road, Chesterfield, Derbys. S40 2PH.
  Resources to support the development of co-ordination and movement skills.
- **Toe by Toe** by Keda Cowling
  Available from 8 Green Road, Baildon, Shipley, W. Yorks. BD17 5HL.

6. Curriculum

Books

Barrs, M. and Thomas, A. (1996) *The Reading Book,* Centre for Language in Primary Education, Webber Row, London SE1 8QW.
Goswami, U. and Bryant, P. (1990) *Phonological Skills and Learning to Read,* Erlbaum, New York.
Gussin-Paley, Vivian has written many books on play including *A Child's Work: The Importance of Play* (2004), University of Chicago Press, Chicago, IL, and *Wally's Stories,* Harvard University Press, Cambridge, MA.
Layton, L., Deeny, R. and Upton, G. (1993) *Sound Practice: Phonological Awareness in the Classroom,* David Fulton, London.
Lloyd, P., Mitchell, H. and Monk, J. (1999) *The Literacy Hour and Language Knowledge: Developing Literacy through Fiction and Poetry,* David Fulton, London.
Reason, R. and Boote, R. (1994) *Helping Children with Reading and Spelling: A Special Needs Manual,* Routledge, London.
Snowling, M.J. (1985) *Children's Written Language Difficulties,* Nelson, London.

Resources

- ***Cloze Encounters*** and ***Write Now***
  Graded cloze exercises and pictures and key words to help with writing.
  Precise Educational, Willowbank House, Golden Valley, Alfreton, Derbys. DE55 4ES.
- **Easy Learn**
  Photocopiable spelling/phonic books from letter sounds through to silent letters.
  Trent House, Fiskerton, Southwell, Notts. NG25 0UH.
- ***The First 100 Words*** by Elaine Doffman (1994)
  Core vocabulary, photocopiable.
  SENTER, Freepost NT 2550, Whitley Bay NE26 1BR.
- **Gamz**
  Swap and fix spelling/phonic card games that the children can play with minimum supervision. Also games on CD-ROM.
  Gamz, 25 Albert Park Road, Malvern, Worcs. WR14 1HW.
- **A Helping Hand for Teachers**
  A phonic spelling programme.
  SENTER, Freepost NT 2550, Whitley Bay NE26 1BR.
- ***Jolly Grammar – The Grammar Handbook 1*** by Sara Wernham and Sue Lloyd (2000)
  Jolly Learning Ltd, Tailours House, High Road, Chigwell, Essex IG7 6Dl.
- **Language Through Drawing and Language Through Reading**

Available through ICAN, 4 Dyers Buildings, Holborn, London EC1N 2QP.

- **Let's Look**
  94 photocopiable masters for visual discrimination activities, pre-reading discrimination exercises.
  LDA, Duke Street, Wisbech, Cambs. PE13 2AE or online at www.instructionalfair.co.uk
- **Let's Spell**
  Five books (Three-letter words, Words that start with a blend, Words that end with a blend, Words that start and end with a blend, Words with double vowels).
  Smart Kids UK Ltd, 169B Main Street, New Greenham Park, Thatcham, Berks. RG19 6HN or online at www.smartkidscatalog.com
- **Phonic Activities 1 & 2**
  Brighter Vision Educational Ltd, Eton House, 18–24 Paradise Road, Richmond, Surrey TW9 1SR.
- **Sound Beginnings**
  LDA, Duke Street, Wisbech, Cambs. PE13 2AE or online at www.instructionalfair.co.uk
- **The Text Checker**
  A quick and easy way of checking the reading age of any text to ensure that it matches pupils' needs.
  The Inclusion Consultancy Ltd, PO Box 11308, Sutton Coldfield B74 4WN or online at www.tic1.co.uk
- **Timesavers Phonics Books 1–6**
  Photocopiable masters
  Precise Educational, Willowbank House, 19 Golden Valley, Riddings, Derbys. DE55 4ES.
- **The Whiz Kids**
  A series of attractive photocopiable books containing story-based exercises including tracking, classification, following instructions, prediction, cloze and deduction.
  Learning Materials Ltd, Dixon Street, Wolverhampton WV2 2BX or online at learning.materials@btinternet.com
- **Write about the picture and story frames**
  From Easy Learn, Trent House, Fiskerton, Southwell, Notts. NG25 0UH.
- **Writing Frames for Infants**
  Photocopiable and CD-ROM
  Belair Publications, Albert House, Apex Business Centre, Boscombe Road, Dunstable, Beds. LU5 4RL or online at www.belair-publications.co.uk
- **Writing Through Role Play**
  Sound Learning, 3 Littleton Business Park, Littleton Drive, Cannock, Staffs. WS12 4TR or online at ww.soundlearning.co.uk for two excellent books with writing ideas for role-play areas.

And I have picked up some real bargains in Pound Shops!
I Can Learn – rhyming cards
Beginning to Read – Silent 'e' card pack

Mathematics

Books/References

Atkinson, S. (ed.) (1992) *Mathematics and Reason,* Hodder & Stoughton, London.
Clausen-May, T. (2005) *Teaching Maths to Pupils with Different Learning Styles,* Paul Chapman.
Cook, G., Jones, L., Murphy, C. and Thumpston, G. (1997) *Enriching Early Mathematical Learning,* Oxford University Press, Oxford.
El-Naggar, O. (1996) *Specific Learning Difficulties in Mathematics: A Classroom Approach,* NASEN Enterprises Ltd, NASEN House, 4/5 Amber Business Village, Amington, Tamworth, Staffs. B77 4RP.
Grauberg, E. (1998) *Elementary Maths and Language Difficulties,* Whurr, Chichester.
MacGregor, H. (2005) *Tom Thumb's Musical Maths,* A&C Black, London.

Resources

- ***A–Z of Maths Games*** by Karen Breitbart
  A selection of simple mathematics games, it contains over 50 photocopy masters and is a really good and useful buy.
  Brilliant Publications, The Old School Yard, Leighton Road, Northall, Dunstable, Beds. LU6 2HA.
- **BBC Video Plus Numbertime**
  BBC Educational Information, BBC White City, London W12 7TS.
- **Easylearn Maths**, Number Books 1–3
  Trent House, Fiskerton, Southwell, Notts. NG25 0UH.
- **Ginn's Abacus scheme**, particularly their Simmering book of short, oral mathematics activities
  Ginn, Linacre House, Jordan Hill, Oxford, OX2 8DP.
- **Maths Now**
  A mathematics series for Key Stages 2 and 3 written with special needs/language difficulties in mind
  John Murray Publishers Ltd, 50 Albemarle Street, London W1X 4BD.
- At Key Stage 1 we have found **Platform Maths** an excellent scheme. It is an activity-based scheme, having no workbooks. A Teacher's Handbook contains detailed lesson plans packed with ideas and activities.
  Nelson Thornes Ltd, Delta Place, 27 Bath Road, Cheltenham, Glos. GL53 7ZZ or online at www.nelsonthornes.com
- **Scottish Primary Maths and Heinemann Maths** are also particularly useful.
  Heinemann, Halley Court, Jordan Hill, Oxford OX2 8EJ.

- **Slavonic abacus**
  The Association of Teachers of Mathematics (ATM) has an explanatory article on the Slavonic abacus on its website and some downloadables: www.atm.org.uk
  Class Creations have a large class-size Slavonic abacus for sale: www.classcreations.com
- **Talking Maths** pictures
  LDA, Duke Street, Wisbech, Cambs. PE13 2AE or online at www.instructionalfair.co.uk

There is a wide range of mathematics resources available from a number of companies and some can be easily made. We have found the following particularly useful:

- A range of counters - buttons, bottle tops, sticks.
- A range of teacher-made number lines and number squares.
- Sandpaper numerals - available from Philip & Tacey Ltd, North Way, Andover, Hants. SP10 5BA.
- Number stamps - we purchased some excellent ones from Kershaws Rubber Stamps, Plane Tree, Goose House Lane, Darwen, BB3 0EH.
- Sumthings - excellent counters, which are on a string rather like rosary beads, so can be moved up and down the string yet hold their position. Available from St Joseph's Workshops, 90 Bagg Lane, Atherton, Manchester.
- Multi-link cubes, unifix or similar with 1–10 trays.
- Cuisenaire rods.
- Logiblocks.
- Dominoes.
- Large dice.
- Beads for threading and pattern cards.
- A set of measuring containers plus everyday containers that the children are familiar with - shampoo bottles, pop bottles, etc.
- Balance scales, weights and a selection of items to weigh including teacher-made parcels. We have two types of parcel - a set of small, same-sized boxes with different items put inside making them different weights and a set of different-sized parcels where some big parcels are very light and some small parcels are very heavy.
- Individual clocks with analogue and digital. These can be simply made by buying or photocopying and laminating analogue clocks then adding a strip of white card at the bottom with two central dots. This can then be used as a whiteboard digital clock.
- One-minute and five-minute timers, a kitchen timer and a stop clock.
- Commercial solid shapes and a set of environmental solid shapes, things the children will be familiar with - cylindrical felt pens, coins/cuboid books, boxes/cubes, Oxo cubes, bricks - to help them make connections between their mathematics shape vocabulary and their world.
- Plastic coins and real coins.

Science

Books/References

- ***The Big Book of Science Rhymes and Chants*** (1991)
  By Jo Ellen Moore and Leslie Tryon
  Available through Scholastic Publications, Villiers House, Clarendon Avenue, Leamington Spa, Warwicks. CV32 5PR.
- **Naturetrek Science Resource books**
  Key Stages 1 and 2. These are excellent for teaching, recording and assessment. There is a new set based on Key Stage 1 books but adapted with new age-appropriate illustrations so they can be used by older pupils with SLI or special needs.
  Naturetrek Educational, St Asaph, Denbighshire, North Wales LL17 0AZ.
- **Scholastic Publications** also produce a range of useful books:
  Seeds and Seedlings
  Pushing and Pulling
  Light and Colour
- ***Science for Children with Learning Difficulties*** (1990)
  Simon and Schuster, London.
- ***Science Sequencing Pictures***
  By Evan Moor - very useful picture sequences of seed to plant, caterpillar to butterfly, etc. This is an American publication so you will need to change some vocabulary, e.g. Fall to Autumn.

Resources

- The **BBC** produces a number of very useful science videos:
  Materials & Their Uses
  Electricity, Light & Sound
  People & Living
  Forces & Weather
  BBC Video Plus, BBC Educational Information, BBC White City, London W12 7TS.

There is a wide range of science resources available from a number of companies and we have access to our mainstream school stock of these but in addition we wouldn't be without:

- a set of toys collected from charity shops, school fairs, etc. that are used during work on forces and motion and electricity;
- a set of lights old and new and reflective toys/ornaments - candles, torches, kaleidoscopes, different mirrors, that is used during work on light;
- a class percussion and music-making set that is used during work on sound;
- a set of items made from different materials both synthetic and natural that is used during work on materials;
- a class gardening kit that is used during work on life and living things.

All the above are used for vocabulary work and in addition we have sets of items for particular vocabulary/concepts:

- rough/smooth
- hard/soft
- wet/dry.

These are ready prepared for teaching and as hands-on displays.

Wider curriculum

Resources

- **A Sense of History Series at Key Stages 1 and 2**
  Pearson, Schools' Division, Harlow, Essex CM20 2YF.
- The **BBC** produces a number of very useful history/geography videos:
  90 Years Ago with Magic Grandad
  Seaside Holidays with Magic Grandad
  Within Living Memory
  Famous Events
  Famous People
  BBC Video Plus, BBC Educational Information, BBC White City, London W12 7TS.
- **The Excellence of Play** by Janet Moyle (1993) Oxford University Press.
- **Guidelines for a Speech and Language Friendly School** by a partnership of educational professionals, QEd, Swindon.
- **Legend into Language**
  By Moira Andrew – Myths and Legends at Key Stages 1 and 2.
  Belair Publications, PO Box 12, Twickenham, Middx. TW1 2QL.
- **Long ago and far away**
  Activities using stories for history and geography at Key Stage 1.
  Developmental Educational Centre, Gillett Centre, 998 Bristol Road, Selly Oak, Birmingham B29 6LE.
- ***Musical Starting Points with Young Children*** by Jean Gilbert (1991)
  Ward Locke, East Grinstead.
- ***Starting with Me*** by Barbara Hume and Annie Sevier (1991)
  Topic ideas for history, geography and RE at Key Stage 1. Belair Publications.
- **Talking History** pictures
  LDA, Duke Street, Wisbech, Cambs. PE13 2AE or online at www.instructionalfair.co.uk
- ***Three Singing Pigs*** by Kaye Umansky (1994)
  Music and traditional stories
  A & C Black, London.

7. Assessment

Books

Law, J., Lindsay, G., Peacey, N., Gascoigne, M., Soloff, N., Radford, J., Band, S., Fitzgerald, L. (2000) *Provision for Children with Speech and Language Needs in England and Wales: Facilitating Communication between Education and Health Services*, London: DfEE.

8. Individual Educational Programmes

Books

Baltaxe, C.A. and Simmons, J.Q. (1990) 'The differential diagnosis of communication disorders in child and adolescent psychopathology', *Topics in Language Disorders* 10, 17–31.

Bateman, B.D. and Herr, C.N. (2003) *Writing Measurable IEP Goals and Objectives*, Attainment, Madison, WI.

Beitchman, J.H. (1985) 'Speech and language impairment and psychiatric risk: toward a model of neurodevelopmental immaturity', *Psychiatry Clinician North America* December, 8(4), 721–35.

Beitchman, J.H., Hood, J. and Inglis, A. (1990) 'Psychiatric risk in children with speech and language disorders', *Journal of Abnormal Child Psychology* 3, 283–96.

Beitchman, J.H., Brownlie, E.B. and Q. Wilson, B. (1996) 'Linguistic impairment and psychiatric disorder: pathways to outcome' in J.H. Beitchman, N.J. Cohen, M.M. Konstantareas and R. Tannock (eds) *Language, Learning and Behavior Disorders: Developmental, Biological and Clinical Perspectives*, Cambridge University Press, New York, pp. 494–514.

Bryan, K. (2004) 'Preliminary study of the prevalence of speech and language difficulties in young offenders', *International Journal of Language and Communication Disorders* 39(3), 391–400.

Cantwell, D.P. and Baker, L. (1985) 'Psychiatric and learning disorders in children with speech and language disorders: a descriptive analysis', *Advances in Learning and Behavioural Disabilities* 4, 29–47.

Cohen, N.J., Menna, R., Vallance, D.D., Barwick, M.A., Im, N. and Horodezky, N.M. (1988a) 'Language, social cognitive processing and behavioural characteristics of psychiatrically disturbed children with previously unidentified and unsuspected language impairments', *Journal of Child Psychology and Psychiatry* 39(6), 853–64.

Gallagher, T.M. (1999) 'Interrelationships among children's language, behaviour and emotional problems', *Topics in Language Disorders* 19, 1–15.

Law, J. and Sivyer, S. (2003) 'Promoting the communication skills of primary schoolchildren excluded from school or at risk of exclusion: an intervention study', *Child Language Teaching and Therapy* 19(1), 1–27.

Melamed, L.E. and Wozniak, J.R. (1999) 'Neuropsychology, language and behaviour' in D. Roger-Adkinson and P. Griffiths (eds)

Communication disorders and children with psychiatric and behavioral disorders. Singular, San Diego, pp. 99–139.
Naylor, M.W., Staskowski, M., Kenney, M.C. and King, C.A. (1994) 'Language disorders and learning disabilities in school-refusing adolescents', *Journal of the American Academy of Child and Adolescent Psychiatry* 33, 1331–7.
Prizant, B.M., Audet, L.R., Burke, G.M., Hummel, L.J., Maher, S.R. and Theodore, G. (1990) 'Communication disorders and emotional/behavioural disorders in children and adolescents', *Journal of Speech and Hearing Disorders* 55, 179–92.
Redmond, S.M. and Rice, M.L. (1998) 'The socio-emotional behaviours of children with SLI: social adaptation or social deviance?' *Journal of Speech, Language and Hearing Research* 41, 688–700.
Tallal, P., Dukette, D. and Curtiss, S. (1989) 'Behavioural/emotional profiles of pre-school language impaired children', *Development and Psychopathology* 1, 51–67.
Tod, J. and Blamires, M. (1999) *IEPs Speech and Language*, David Fulton, London.
War-Leeper, G. (2002) 'The relationship between behaviour and language disorders: patterns of language impairment and implication for management.' Conference address, OSSTF Conference, Ontario.
Willinger, U., Brunner, E., Diendorf-Radner, G., Sams, J., Sirsch, U. and Eisenwort, B. (2003) 'Behaviour in children with language development disorders', *Canadian Journal of Psychiatry* 48, 407–614.

Appendix 1

Books

Crystal, D. (1989) *Listen to Your Child: A Parent's Guide to Children's Language*, Penguin, Harmondsworth.
Sheridan, M., Frost, M. and Sharma, A. (1997) *From Birth to Five Years*, Routledge, London.

Appendix 3

Book

Nash-Wortham, M. (1993) *Phonic Rhyme Time*, Stourbridge, Robinswood Press.

CPSIA information can be obtained
at www.ICGtesting.com
Printed in the USA
LVHW061035300123
738198LV00006B/149

9 780826 491039